WESTERN MORNING VIEWS

WESTERN MORNING VIEWS

Selections from

The Western Morning News

1984–1985

Compiled by
Crispin Gill & James Mildren

HARBOUR BOOKS : DARTMOUTH
1985

First published in Great Britain by
Harbour Books, 12 Fairfax Place,
Dartmouth, Devon TQ6 9AE

British Library Cataloguing in Publication Data

Western morning views : selections from the
Western morning news 1984–1985.
I. Gill, Crispin II. Mildren, James
III. Western morning news
072'.358

ISBN 0–907906–07–9

Filmset in 10/12pt Plantin by Photoprint, Torquay.
Printed and bound in Great Britain by
A. Wheaton & Co. Ltd., Exeter.

Editors' Note

In the course of a year a newspaper prints a vast amount of material. This is an anthology culled from the pages of the Western Morning News for one year, spring 1984 to the end of winter 1985. In some measure it reflects the short-lived editorship of Brian MacArthur, who brought many changes to the newspaper but fundamentally aimed at developing what might be called the background, the spirit, the feel behind what was going on.

Even more important than the influence of one man in the long life of a newspaper, it was the 125th anniversary of the paper's foundation. The jubilee and the centenary have been celebrated in their time and, in these days of change and new ideas, an old institution—and the Western Morning News is nothing less in the West Country—needs to mark its milestones.

Two of us have been keeping cuttings, day after day, from the paper during this period. My own service with the Western Morning News began in 1934; James Mildren is of the post-war vintage but he rejoices in or suffers from the same old-fashioned ideas of devotion and loyalty that mark my older generation. At the end of the time we had a joint session matching our selections, with the inevitable heavy discard, and then he took the resulting pile away for the final selection and placing in order.

We tried to cover everything, from leaders and letters to the editor, to nature notes, the news columns and the sports pages. We took bits and pieces here and there from what might be called the gossip writers, the columnists who cover all aspects of their subject or stretch of country. We tried to touch on the great local issues and the little incidentals. In short, we tried to convey the flavour of the paper.

On me fell the final task of cutting to size, and there are very few articles indeed here that run to the length in which they appeared in the paper. They were all cut drastically so that we could cover the widest possible field and the greatest number of contributors. Some are staff men and women, some outside contributors.

All we hope is that we have given a fair sample of what James says is called "The Paper"; what we irreverent characters in the production team used to call "The Daily Miracle". And we hope you find some pleasure in these pages.

Crispin Gill

Contents

Summer

Autumn

Winter

Illustrations

Facing page 99
4930 "Hagley Hall" and 7819 "Hinton Manor" climbing Dainton bank between Totnes and Newton Abbot with the "Great Western Limited".
Photo: Mark S. Wilkins
H.M.S. Torquay, the frigate built in 1956, paying her farewell visit to Torbay on being retired from the active fleet.
Photo: Torbay News Agency

Facing page 114
H.R.H. Princess Anne on a recent visit to the West Country.

Facing page 115
Truro Cathedral enveloped in a snow storm.
The round houses of Veryan keeping out the devil.
Photo: Bob Roskrow

Foreword

Cyril Connolly, the author of at least one masterpiece (the autobiography *Enemies of Promise*) described literature as 'the art of writing something that will be read twice, journalism what will be grasped at once'. In part, this has always seemed to me a reflection by Connolly on the amount of time he devoted to what one commentator has called 'reviewage' rather than to the writing of his own books. All the same, as a literary journalist, and one of the finest of his generation, he was a member of a profession including at one time or another such distinguished practitioners as Dr. Johnson, Dickens, Arnold Bennett, Bernard Shaw, George Orwell, H. L. Mencken and Chekhov. And, in the imponderable alchemy of writing, who is to know whether a piece written to be grasped at once may not also survive to be admired and re-read a hundred times or more? It's all part of the fun in an exacting game.

I have discovered a curious and pleasant characteristic of journalists to be their invariable extreme modesty over the literary value of their work. Perhaps, I can hear you say, this is because they have plenty to be modest about. But I cannot agree. The ability to produce, in an often paralysingly brief period of time, a piece of writing clear, balanced, to the point, engineered to an exact number of words and often produced under conditions varying only from the chaotic to the hopeless, demands the sort of nerve, skill and precision that would drive many a novelist, playwright, poet or biographer prematurely to the cemetery or crematorium.

Only a lunatic sets out with the express purpose of writing a masterpiece. Furthermore, it has never been my belief that long periods of gestation, of endless pruning and polishing, necessarily produce something worth reading once, let alone twice. Some writers are four-minute milers; some not. All that really matters, be it something written in twenty minutes or twenty years, is whether the writer has been lucky enough (and luck, as well as technique, plays an important part) to inject into the work that mysterious element which gently and insistently draws us to it again and again for recreation and refreshment.

The compilers' judicious selection of work from *The Western Morning News* offers this delicious opportunity. Reading over the text, I have made many a delightful discovery; re-encountered more than one contribution I had piously intended preserving at the time of its original publication.

I remember Henry Williamson saying that he loved regional and local newspapers best of all because he felt they reflected so much more truthfully and accurately than their big metropolitan brothers the lives and natures of the communities they served. I am certain he was right. What we call 'the west', of course, like every other division of our crowded and infinitely surprising islands, is another country. Very properly, it defies precise geographical demarcation as much as a definitive analysis of its own particular ambience, character, flavour.

To each of us, then, is his or her own special vision of the West Country. But as a guide, a pointer to the inner life of an always secret place, and secret people—as a work that, as it were, catches a most wonderfully mixed community to the life, and in the sharpest and most telling focus at certain moments in its history—I commend this splendidly entertaining and illuminating anthology. It may be the first in the newspaper's century and a quarter of life, but I certainly hope it will not be the last.

It was the great Norwegian dramatist Henrik Ibsen who declared that the torture of animals by scientists was inexcusable. 'Let them make their experiments on journalists and politicians,' he went on. Leaving the politicians aside, no-one who has enjoyed what follows as much as I have could in all heart agree.

Charles Causley
Launceston, Cornwall

THE ALBERT MEMORIAL.

November 1884. An attempt to horsewhip Albert Groser, editor of The Western Morning News, at the bottom of George Street, Plymouth. The figure on the pavement carries the rival newspaper, The Western Daily Mercury. Probably this cartoon is from the humorous Plymouth journal of the time, the Western Figaro.

125 Years Old

One hundred and twenty five years ago today [3 January 1985] The Western Morning News made its first appearance. It would have appeared on 1 January 1860, had that not been a Sunday, and the following Monday was taken up putting that first issue together.

It was the first English daily paper published west of Bristol; indeed it was the sixth in England outside London. From the first it was designed to serve all the Westcountry, and the first two issues contain advertisements from newsagents in Hayle, Truro, St. Austell, Torquay, Newton Abbot, Totnes, Falmouth, Teignmouth and Plymouth. There were other advertisements and news items from Exeter, Tavistock, and Launceston.

The times were right for such a venture. In 1859, the year the paper was planned, the Royal Albert Bridge across the Tamar was opened, providing a main railway line from London to Truro; a smaller line went on to Penzance. In 1859, too, the Plymouth-Tavistock railway line had opened, and other branch lines were under construction or planned. So news packets could be brought to Plymouth rapidly, and the newspapers sent out. From railheads the newspapers went on by mail coaches, and North Devon could be reached by rail by changing trains at Exeter.

The electric telegraph was a recent invention, although messages were still sent by morse code. The first news item ever sent by the telegraph in this country had told The Times in August 1844 of the birth of Queen Victoria's second son, and, in 1855, the Daily Telegraph took its name from the new invention. Also it was the country's first penny paper.

This price was made possible first by the abolition of a tax on advertisements, then the end of the tax on newspapers, and in 1859 it was firmly (and correctly) expected that the tax on paper would end in 1860.

So, the first Western Morning News was a penny paper, of four pages. The first page was given up to advertisements, in the fashion of the day (and The Western Morning News did not move news onto the front page until January 1, 1949 when Noel Vinson began his editorship). There were more advertisements on page two and the back page; so many advertisements had been submitted that there was not room for all.

In 1860 there were many weekly papers in Devon and Cornwall, including two strong ones in Plymouth. There had been many others which had come and gone in a year or two, many of them little more than propaganda sheets to advance the ideas of their owners. William Hunt, an East Devon man with newspaper experience in London, had come to Plymouth and worked on several of these short-lived ventures. He had sickened of the eternal bickerings in print between them and had become librarian of Plymouth Public Library, which flourishes still as Plymouth Proprietary Library.

In the Library one day in 1859 he was introduced by Alderman Alfred Rooker, a Tavistock-born solicitor who had become leader of the Liberals on Plymouth Town Council, to a young man from Bath, William Saunders; later he met Saunders's brother-in-law, Edward

Spender, who had married a Plymouth girl. Both had settled in Plymouth and were looking for business opportunities.

Among ideas discussed between them and Rooker was the idea of a daily newspaper which would rise above all the petty party battles. The idea developed, premises were found at the bottom of Bedford Street, looking down Frankfort Street, and on the third day of the New Year the new paper was launched.

Very soon Hunt found the pressure of work in Plymouth—he would end his "day" at 4.30 a.m., be back in the office by 9.30 a.m. and just take a couple of hours off in the late afternoon—told on his health to such an extent that he had to retire.

When Spender moved to London permanently, one of the reporters, Albert Groser, became editor. He was expert at using the developing railway system to distribute the paper; under him it grew rapidly. The paper suffered in 1878 when Spender, on holiday from London, went swimming with his two sons at Whitsands near Plymouth and all three were swept out to sea and drowned. A monument on Tregonhawke cliffs stands as a memorial and a warning still.

When the paper was launched, Plymouth was flourishing and Devonport growing apace; the two, with Stonehouse, made the Three Towns a continuous conurbation, the seventh largest in England outside London. The Royal Navy was adapting to steam power and the Steam Yard—now known as North Yard—had not been long opened. Throughout the West farming flourished. The West Cornish mines were beginning to fade out but those of East Cornwall and the Tamar Valley were keeping up the county's overall prosperity.

The Western Morning News had its rival. Isaac Latimer, a staunch and outspoken radical Liberal, had launched the Western Daily Mercury from Plymouth six months after the Morning News. The papers were to share some facilities—like special trains—but mostly it was a full-blooded rivalry.

As the century moved to its close the economic climate was changing. Mines bottomed out until only a handful were left. Farming was in the doldrums from 1870 onwards. After the 1914–18 war it was clear that there was no room for two morning papers in the Westcountry, and both papers were suffering.

EDITORS

1860–63	**Edward Spender**
1863–95	**Albert Groser**
1895–97	**T. H. Barrow**
1897–1902	**Robert Michie**
1902–21	**T. Canning Bailey**
1921–48	**James L. Palmer**
1949–74	**Noel A. T. Vinson**
1975–84	**John Carter**
1984–85	**Brian MacArthur**
1985–	**Colin Davison**

In 1920 Sir Leicester Harmsworth, a younger brother of Lord Northcliffe, founder of the Daily Mail and indeed of modern journalism, bought first The Western Morning News and then The Mercury. The papers were amalgamated. The Western Morning News offices and printing works in George Street, opposite the Theatre Royal (where they had been since 1865) were closed and the Mercury building, in Frankfort Street, became the headquarters of the joint paper.

The old building, which still had the lofts in the roof where pigeons once brought messages from out-of-town reporters, was rebuilt between 1936 and 1938. It survived the bombing and fires of the blitz, though at times all main services were cut and the paper had to be produced first at Exeter and later at Tavistock. It never missed a single wartime edition and, when the new city was rebuilt, The Western Morning News building stayed; to this day its front is not properly on the line of New George Street.

"We have set before ourselves a high standard", stated the editorial of that first issue. That standard has been the aim of The Western Morning News ever since. With new ideas, new technology and the determination not only to reflect the events, but the interests and the ideas of the Westcountry, the newspaper hopes to go on serving the South-West, and striving for its best interests.

Crispin Gill

Where is the West?

Where does the Westcountry begin? The answer, of course, depends on from where one is looking. For some Londoners, Bayswater is a long way west, never mind Basingstoke. For the Ministry men in Whitehall, looking at their tidy little maps parcelling up the whole country, it is all quite clear. The South-West Region begins where the South-East Region ends.

Never mind the fact that, coming on the straight road home, we people from down along are considered to be in the Westcountry almost as soon as we come down off Salisbury Plain. Further north, on the A40 to Gloucester and South Wales, this wonderful transition happens just 22 miles west of Oxford, with Cheltenham still 20 miles further on.

In Burford, the last parish in Oxfordshire, one is lumped with Norwich and Dover and Greater London itself, in South-East England. Just past a clump of trees, into Barrington, the first parish of Gloucestershire, the Civil Servant is in the world of West Penwith and wildest Exmoor, the South-West. Even Exeter is more than a hundred miles away, as that celebrated crow flies.

One must look the other way to get the proper perspective, but even then there are as many answers as there are people down here. Crossing Newlyn Bridge is a bit risky for anyone from the west of it; after all Penzance is a mortal wicked big town. All people from West Penwith square their shoulders a little if they go east of Truro, and once east of St. Austell they hear the locals beginning to talk like Devon people. The sing-song has gone out of the voices.

Crossing the Tamar is a moment when all Cornishmen tighten their belts, and the West Devon man worries when he gets over the Exe. The crest of the Blackdown Hills on the A38, or the little River Yarty on the A30, are other key points. This was the frontier of the great Celtic tribe of Damnonnia, who occupied all Devon and Cornwall before the Saxons began to push west, and these tangled hills and valleys were the frontier.

But Taunton is reassuring, like Dorchester; it feels proper, comfortable. Glastonbury and Wells are all right. Further south along the frontier Yeovil must be on our side, but this is real border country. Not far on, just past Yeovilton, we see the Cadbury hills rising out of the marshes, and we know that the archaeologists, indeed antiquarians for centuries past, have placed Camelot here.

From this hilltop Arthur could defy the Saxons, retreating back into the marshes and even lose himself in Athelney if he was pressed. There he had all the Westcountry at his back; he had no worry.

So, perhaps, we can settle for the heights of Mendip, the marshes of central Somerset and the tangled hills of Dorset, as our defence against England, our ultimate frontier.

But the Westcountry is not a precise term. It is not to be defined by Civil Service decree or constrained by county boundaries. It is a mental thing, a reaction, a response to a stimulus. One might say it has all the exhilaration, all the infuriation, all the intoxication, of any normal love affair.

9 March 1985 **Editorial**

SPRING

Birdsong in the February dawn

On a Sunday morning at this time of year it is tempting to snuggle deeper into the bedclothes and take an extra hour or two in bed, but on this occasion the persistent singing of our friendly neighbourhood song thrush persuaded me to rise at my normal time and find out what gave the thrush such good reason for its cheerful song.

It was just the sort of morning thrushes seem to like best—mild and misty! Just the morning one would have thought for seeking snails and worms which had not yet concealed themselves after their night's activities. But instead, every song thrush in every garden seemed intent on outdoing his neighbours in a frenzied outpouring of song. Not just thrushes, I soon realised, but wrens too, seemed totally absorbed in this early morning territorial battle. I decided to get dressed and go for a walk before breakfast, and find out just who else was involved in the February dawn chorus.

It was not long before I heard the liquid bubbling cry of a curlew, followed at once by a rising and then descending whistle, which told me that the "curlew" call had, in fact, come from a starling—one of Nature's most accomplished mimics, which was perched on an overhead wire rehearsing his entire repertoire, including even the distinctive whistle of a golden oriole. I wondered where he had learnt that one. The answer is probably from previous generations of starlings, for many of the species' imitations have now become, as it were, traditional.

David Hunt
Isles of Scilly

A tragic piece this, for in the very edition in which it appeared was the report that David Hunt, the young but already renowned ornithologist of the Isles of Scilly, had died after being mauled by a tiger while leading a party of bird-watchers in an Indian game reserve. **Editor**

"Satellite spying on my spuds"

A farmer claimed last night that the Potato Marketing Board has been spying on his crop by satellite.

Mr. Bill Coles asked an inspector how they knew he had broken Common Market regulations by growing too many potatoes and was told: "We have other ways than aircraft of photographing your farm." He then pointed at the sky.

"I thought he was pulling my leg and asked him if he meant a satellite," said Bill. "He nodded and he was quite serious.

"What he said really knocked me back. It all smacks of Big Brother having a satellite watching your potato crop."

A spokesman for the Potato Marketing Board at Exeter, Mr. Glen Burrows, said "The technology does exist, although it is very expensive. It would be far easier to photograph crops from an aircraft, a technique which is often used."

Now Bill, who farms around 200 acres at Salcombe Regis and Harcombe, near Sidmouth, is waiting to hear if he will be penalised.

"Like all farmers, I am only allowed to grow so many potatoes and if I grow too many and break my EEC quota I have to pay £70 a hectare for the privilege of growing them.

"I did grow more than I declared, but you never expected them to have a satellite watching your farm."

Ironically, due to a delay in building a new potato store, Bill, 46, was unable to dig the potatoes until after Christmas and by then frost had destroyed 80 per cent of them.

Wanted: major centre for Cornish art

Cornwall has long attracted and fostered the development of artistic talent. It has much to do with a unique, often exhilarating, landscape and something to do with a centuries-old harmony of place and people.

Few other parts of the country could merit an exhibition such as that now being held at the Tate Gallery in London. This centres on one of Cornwall's main colonies of artists at St. Ives and well portrays the explosion of creative energy which has taken place there in post-war years. There is also a major exhibition at the Newlyn Orion Gallery of Newlyn painters, which also opened this week.

The Tate display will help to ensure that the St. Ives artists continue to get the recognition which is their due. But, for the most part, the visitors poring over Hepworth sculptures, Leach pots and Lanyon paintings will be outsiders. It is a fair presumption that not many Westcountrymen will make the trip to the Capital specifically to see this important exhibition.

There is a good deal for Cornish people to be proud of there. But those who plead poverty or lack of time to travel do have a point. Selected works by local artists should, where possible, be displayed close to the settings which provided inspiration. The criticism is partly answered by a smattering of separate initiatives, such as the Newlyn gallery showing contemporary art, and displays of local work at Falmouth and Penzance. There is also an important outpost in the form of the Hepworth museum at St. Ives, run by the Tate.

But what surely is lacking is a major centre which can show all the strands together. Cornwall should have a museum of modern art to provide a permanent exhibition for its abundant creative contribution. It would be a draw for local people and for visitors alike. What better place to house it than in Truro?

16 February 1985 **Leader**

The absent birds

Since I commented on the unusually small number of birds that had come to our bird table this winter, I have had confirmation that this has been a general experience.

I have not only heard from local naturalists, but some of you have been kind enough to write from various parts of the South-West to report the absence of their usual visitors.

I was a little surprised that the first heavy frosts did not change the picture greatly. But the first snowfall brought my feathered friends back in their hordes.

Obviously the excellent berry and seed crops and the extended period of insect activity had kept them well satisfied until the New

Year and, even when it became very cold, turning up the fallen leaves in the hedgerows must have been a good source of rations.

A white blanket shut this off and blue tits, great tits, robins, blackbirds and hedge sparrows arrived in hordes. Although our usual squad of finches has yet to turn up, we did have most unusual visitors today.

Barbara told me to look out of the living room window and there was a pair of snipe parading about underneath the bird table. I think what had attracted them was a strip of bare ground I had cleared of snow.

From the air this would have looked like a piece of soft earth warmed by an underground spring which these birds look for in hard weather so that they can probe for their favourite feed of earthworms and grubs.

Their beaks are well adapted for this purpose and look far too big for their owners. This, added to an almost ducklike waddle, make snipe look almost ungainly on the ground.

A sudden fright made the snipe take off and they immediately became the epitome of grace and power. They climbed at three times the speed of a blackbird that flew at the same instant, and jinked swiftly in a wide circle down to a rush-lined spring outside the garden.

Bob Holmes

Jump–not me!

I find it odd that parachuting should appeal to so many people.

Dunkeswell Airfield in Devon has a sky-diving centre offering two-day courses for £42.

The Mayors of Tiverton and Barnstaple are to make parachute jumps for charity. One is 47 and the other 64.

Good luck to them and all parachute jumpers. There was a time when I spent many, many hours quietly praying that I wouldn't have to use a parachute.

Crossing the road is sufficiently dangerous for me these days.

John Theobald

The best bad painter

Painter Robert Lenkiewicz operates by the simple creed that there are no laws or rules in the business of living.

Thirty years' study of philosophy and metaphysics has convinced him that the only justification for life is for it to be as full, rich, and creative as possible.

That so few achieve this ideal is, he says, entirely the fault of the family structure—"one of the social diseases of our time."

"Many things kill—drink, cigarettes—but there are psychological deaths through human relationships. Two people who are attracted should not become each other's property, yet children are educated in the belief that they have to marry the first acned youth they meet and live in the first squalid hutch they come across. Within a few years they are surrounded by screaming brats and alcohol."

Lenkiewicz maintains that a woman of 30 has an emotional age of 12, a man of 30 an emotional age of three.

"Would you put children of this age together and expect them to make a good relationship?" he asked.

What saddens him is the effect of a joyless environment on infants, who he believes learn more in the first three years than in the rest of their lives. "They will pick up inhibition and repression and be crushed by it."

To Lenkiewicz there is no better legacy to offer a child than a "yes" attitude to life from parents who are creatively active and feel their own lives are rich.

He trusts that he and the mothers of his own children have been able to pass on this legacy. He does not offer the conventional father role to these many children but says they share "a rich relationship in which everything is discussed. We are totally open. We learn that only by valuing ourselves can we value others."

His background may help explain the strength of his views. He was born in London in 1942 to Jewish refugee parents, shortly after they had escaped from the holocaust.

Most of their families perished in Belsen and Auschwitz but the Lenkiewicz couple were luckier. They managed to flee from Russia, with Mrs. Lenkiewicz hidden in a sack on a boat.

Much of the family information was washed away in the holocaust but what Lenkiewicz did learn was appropriately dramatic—his father was a rabbi and horse-breaker, his mother originally a German baroness, whose father was court painter to mad King Ludwig of Bavaria.

He trained at St. Martin's School of Art and at the Royal Academy, from which he was expelled ("something to do with a girl sitting on my shoulders").

It was the beginning of his "Albert Schweitzer phase" which was to last for 25 years. After he moved to Plymouth—a decision which he says was governed by instinct—he found himself eventually with nine warehouses accommodating more than a hundred of the city's alcoholics. He withdrew from it all when the average age of the alcoholics dropped from 60 to 40 and their company became dangerous.

Now he confines his interest to some twenty old friends fallen on hard times and an annual Christmas dinner at the bus station.

All the same, his overriding desire has always been to paint everyone and everything on the largest possible canvas.

His Barbican mural on Elizabethan philosophy is now something of an embarrassment. It is his most famous work but he did it only because he likes working on a large scale.

His greatest pleasure in painting is thinking and the energy it demands.

Lenkiewicz does not sell his paintings and has a low regard for his own work.

"There are only four significant painters every 100 years and I am not one of them. But I regard myself as the best bad painter I know," he says.

Gloria Schofield

A real drought could be on the way

It has been said that Britain doesn't have a climate, it just has weather. The variations we have experienced in the past 14 months certainly bear this out.

January, 1984 was generally mild, but stormy, with occasional icy days. The main feature was exceptionally heavy rainfall which brought considerable flooding. This was followed by a reasonably wet February. Hopes of an early spring were dashed by a cold March and cold early April, but by the end of that month it was hot and dry. A generally hot, dry summer followed.

Although water supplies ran short, the trees seemed able to tap reserves left in the ground from the heavy winter rain, and although grass growth was restricted, livestock kept in splendid condition and harvested crops were of excellent quality and above average yield. There was a bountiful crop of wild berries and nuts as there were no frosts at blossom time and ripening conditions were good.

Autumn and early winter were exceptionally mild so that at the end of the year grass was still green and growing. Early in January I noticed that the buds on many plants were beginning to swell and fresh soft leaves were pushing through on many plants.

It is not unusual for January and February to be cold, but usually in such a spell, a blanket of snow provides some protection. This year we suffered some of the lowest temperatures we have ever recorded with the ground completely bare. Within a couple of days the frost was several inches deep into the soil. Livestock with shelter from the wind always do well in cold, dry weather but there was unusual damage to some forms of plant life.

Never before have I seen primrose leaves burnt to shrivelled fragments and many of my garden polyanthus of an exceptionally hardy strain have been killed off, together with aubretia and a number of shrubs such as ceanothus. I was glad that I always prune my roses late as any buds which had started to grow were blasted.

I felt very sorry for the purchasers of the hundreds of roses and shrubs on sale in various stores before Christmas. Packed in polythene bags and kept under warm conditions, they had been stimulated into soft premature growth. These tender shoots must now be black and even if new buds sprout, the plants must have been desperately weakened. There is no doubt that the best shrub to buy is one dug straight from a nursery bed in the open.

Looking at our daily rainfall recordings, I am concerned to see that our rainfall from October, 1984 to February, 1985 totals only 22.89in., compared with 30.35in. from October, 1983 to February, 1984. Remembering last year's water shortage, I wonder if we could be in for a real drought this year—or will a wet summer keep us refreshed, but depress farmers and holidaymakers?

Despite the severity of the cold only a few weeks ago, new life is springing up everywhere. Every day more hazel catkins sway in the breeze and the hedges are spangled with the silver plumes of sallow and the stark white blossom of blackthorn. A green bloom is spreading across the fields which were yellowed by frost and on every patch of bare ground tiny seedlings of various plants are springing into life.

Bob Holmes

Salmon dearth in Salar's river

The best worker in Europe
Is only six-inch long
You thought he'd be a bigger chap?
Wait till you hear my song, my dears,
Wait till you hear my song.

So begins a sad tribute to the salmon by Poet Laureate Ted Hughes, his latest poem written to launch an appeal in Scotland today for the Atlantic Salmon Trust.

"Wait till you hear my song" is a fitting chorus for the shanty-style verse from a man who knows only too well the plight of this noble fish.

For on the River Torridge—setting for Henry Williamson's classic novel Salar the Salmon—which runs close to his North Devon home, their future is desperate.

Just 30 years ago it was renowned throughout Europe as one of the top venues for catching spring salmon, the big mature fish which begin their time-honoured return upriver to the tributaries of their birth at the start of each season.

In 1954, there were 900 salmon caught by rodsmen, most during the early upstream run.

By last year, the numbers caught had dropped to 24; but this year, three weeks since the season officially started, the salmon are nowhere to be found.

Not a single fish has been landed and the rodsmen have already given up hope. The scarcity of salmon is no longer just a cause for local concern, it is a frightening indictment.

For the ultimate judges of pollution control and our supposed care for the environment are not water board scientists with test tubes and samples, but the salmon themselves.

If the salmon no longer return to a river, it is choked and dying.

Raw sewage is pumped daily into the river at its mouth in Bideford, then further upstream many headwaters have effectively died because careless farmers have allowed toxic agricultural discharges to leak into the water systems.

The consequences are two-fold. In the tributaries clogged with poisonous farm waste, young salmon of up to three years old are killed before they have a chance to grow strong enough for their first migration to the rich Icelandic feeding grounds.

The damage to these young fish can never be accurately calculated, not until the mature fish return from the Atlantic to spawn.

And even those large fish which do return to the estuary are turning back from the polluted Torridge as they encounter a river filthy with sewage.

It is believed that they are turning instead to the River Taw, which shares the same estuary mouth yet diverts through Barnstaple—in the opposite direction to Bideford's sewage outfall.

This is not elementary theory, it is a fact proven by catches of salmon on the Taw in these first weeks of the season. A beautiful 25-pounder was landed on the season's first day, March 1. In the following three days, 11 fine specimens were caught.

At last, alarmed by the salmon's decline—and by public pressure—the South West Water Authority is taking action.

An urgent study to "evaluate the state of the river" is currently under way. "It's the most intensive effort we are making on any river in the region," said a spokesman.

Tim Metcalfe

Truro; changed but unchanging

One of the best views of Truro is that from Kenwyn churchyard, with its lovely old lych-gate, clusters of Celtic crosses, massive yew trees and drifts of delicate snowdrops.

To the left is the rolling countryside of the Idless Valley, criss-crossed by hazel hedgerows heavy with catkins.

But, straight in front, framed by Brunel's mighty viaduct, dominated by the cathedral with its trio of spires, and with the river snaking silver in the sunlight, the city lies below, nestling snugly in the valley.

From here it looks exactly as it did 40 years ago in those leather-satcheled, blue-blazered, Just William days of boyhood.

Yet, just as distance is said to lend enchantment, so, too, does it tend to blur reality.

The fact is the city has changed, not, happily, beyond all recognition, but dramatically in parts and subtly in others.

Today's Truro is tidily trim, and with just a touch of "with it" trendiness.

Its narrow streets—one so small it has the rather vulgar name of Squeeze Guts Alley—are peppered with smart boutiques and salted with little shops tucked into tiny mews.

There are, it seems, a score of such establishments now to cater for Cornish sartorial sensibilities, from the stylishly elegant to the cheekily chic—a froth of frilly fashion.

One such emporium sums it up with a wry sense of humour. It trades under the title of "Granny Wouldn't Like It."

They are probably wrong. Granny would have loved it, but she never had the opportunity to wear such clothes.

Mind you, Truro has always had another kind of style. Any place that has a cathedral, a river—three to be precise—cobbled streets—a Victorian granite-built municipal building complete with handsome clock tower, and a sweep of Georgian gracefulness such as Lemon Street, is bound to possess a certain charisma.

Time, and all the changes that have taken place with its passing, might have rippled the lake, but the essential character of Truro remains unaltered.

So, for someone who has spent nearly 30 years away from the city of his birth, what are the changes to startle the retina of memory when you return for the occasional visit?

First and foremost, I suppose, it is the way the quayside has changed. Boscawen Bridge and Quay Park as I remember them—a spot where adventurous kids dived into the river from the parapets of the bridge—have virtually disappeared.

Remnants remain, but not the park as such, with its sunhouse, and turnstiles, a clicking entrance whereby to catch the pleasure boats about to chug on a sedate sail down the winding densely wooded banked River Fal.

They were swallowed up to feed the appetite of that glutinous beast the motor car as highway engineers cut a terraced swathe of dual carriageway from Tregols Road to the top of Falmouth Road and called it Morlaix Avenue in honour of Truro's French twin in Brittany.

The other area that has altered spectacularly is around High Cross and Pydar Street, and here it is that the old and the new really have been forced to live cheek-by-jowl.

Space had to be found for the big stores essential to the business life of a city which the official guide diplomatically describes as Cornwall's "head town" and in the process there have been some casualties.

The fine old Post Office building was one, and the little garden there before the West Front of the cathedral—with its rose window and 200-foot high twin towers and spires—has been dug up and paved over.

But as far as I could recall, most of the splendid buildings remain, like the elegant Assembly Rooms, its warm Bath stone construction said to make up one of the best Georgian houses in Truro, and that very different, but mighty monument to benefactor Passmore Edwards that is the public library.

Although supermarkets and building society branches have replaced landmarks like the impressive Red Lion Hotel and the quaint West Briton building where journalistic milk-teeth were first cut, Truro's main street still looks and feels much as it always did.

Change there has been aplenty, but there is still the ambience of Truro being geared for today but mindful of yesteryear.

Perhaps I am just a little prejudiced, but I make no apologies for that.

Derek Lean

Training for the Good Life

The idea of having a small piece of land and becoming self-sufficient is something most people think is a good idea, but never do anything about.

During the 1970s the idea of self-sufficiency hit a boom time when television programmes like "The Good Life" sparked off more interest.

But at Dartington, the dream of an outdoor life has become a reality. Men and women interested in becoming self-sufficient or wanting to set up small holdings sign up for courses, so they can have a taste of the practical side of life before they jump feet first into a venture that may not work.

The Yarner Trust at Beacon Farm has been running since 1978 and many students of all ages have benefited by its help.

The students help to farm about 20 acres and learn every aspect of running a small holding, from keeping cattle and pigs to growing produce and learning about soil.

Mr. Eric Clarke, director and project manager, said that the Trust tries to make a practical contribution to the growing interest in small-scale mixed farming and rural co-operative self-reliant community life.

"Initially we make available to people a thorough and realistic training in the rudiments of such a way of life, demonstrating the scope for individual fulfilment.

"For people wanting to learn smallholding there can be no substitute for living and working on the land. Experience is essential before committing yourself to the responsibilities of land and animals, and the management of a holding.

"By devoting our time and energy to practising the craft of smallholding, we can bring a wholeness and sense of fulfilment to our lives."

The Trust's farm is run as a small traditional mixed farm of about 20 acres. It has many different types of crops, including wheat, oats and barley, and roots. All are organically grown.

Eric said: "During the summer we grow tomatoes and aubergines in a poly tunnel and this summer we were able to sell £300 worth. In the winter the tunnel is used for growing winter lettuce, chinese cabbage and mizuna, which is Japanese mustard."

One student who was interested in herbs developed a herb garden, and this has been left for future students to expand.

On the livestock side there are goats, 20 ewes, four breeding sows and three South Devons. There are 50 free-range chickens which are being fattened for Christmas.

Janet Wooster

A day in the life of the Theatre Royal

It is a grey day, the pavements still wet from the night's rain. Royal Parade yawns awake as a trickle of traffic swishes through the empty city.

Seven o'clock: A small unseen army of cleaners re-engage their daily battle in the empty offices and corridors of the Theatre Royal, Plymouth. They are the "advance troops" who go to work before the battalions of workers from other departments arrive. The vacuum cleaners probe the two theatres and public foyers, while a back-up weaponry of polishers, mops and brushes briskly defeat the dust for another day.

Eight o'clock: Keith Clayton takes up position as stage door-keeper in a strategically placed reception office at the back of the theatre. Here messages cascade around him like confetti and he can scarcely complete a sentence before a new face appears with a request or inquiry.

"It's all about people here. If you didn't have some sort of rapport this place wouldn't get off the ground. We try to make life easier for the company. That keeps them happy and then they can go on stage and give a better performance. It's a round robin . . ." said Keith during a brief gap between the endless oscillation of customers to and from his counter.

Nine o'clock: Things are beginning to buzz. Switchboard operator David Bennett arrives. Keith plugs in the tea-making machine again.

This is the first day of band rehearsals and the musicians for Wind In The Willows are starting to drift in. First to arrive is the sax player. A card arrives with the words "Thank You For Being The Fabbest Stage Door People In The World!" written across it.

Theatre Royal general manager Andrew Welch, businessman-suited and carrying a briefcase, pops his head around the stage door with a cheery "Good morning" before climbing the stairs to his office. A cleaner trailing an industrial mobile vacuum cleaner behind her picks a cautious way through the growing stage-door congestion.

Ten o'clock: The front of house doors are opened by the duty commissionaire. The box office and buttery are ready to do business. The BOCS computerised ticket system is a far cry from the inked-in X's and books of tickets on the old-style seating plan.

In the auditorium artistic director Roger Redfarn and lighting designer Andrew A. Gardner are lighting the set. It might take five minutes to plot a sequence which will blend before the audiences' eyes in seconds.

The boys in the band have taken over the board room. Instead of committees and agendas, it's foot-tapping musical rebellion with a rousing account of Poop Poop! Musical director Barry Westcott is ironing out any problems with his players before the principal performers join them for rehearsals in the afternoon.

On stage, director Roger Redfarn has just crawled out of Mole's hole on the edge of the river bank. "I have to do it all," he says, a trifle breathy, "Then, when the actors come on and say they can't do this or that I say 'but I have done it'."

He has a check Rupert Bear scarf knotted around his neck and seems to be effortlessly coasting through the inevitable chaos as the production's jigsaw pieces are gradually meshed together. For peace of mind he tries not constantly to remind himself that the first show of this world premiere is only two days away.

As noon approaches life in the kitchen heats up apace from simmering to just off the boil. Head chef John Gorrell is responsible for serving the requirements of the restaurant, buttery circle bar and the actors' Green Room.

He has just made the soup of the day and is now busy with curry and roasting the beef. The next job for John and his staff of five will be preparing the sauces, and then the sweet trolley.

Cooking of a different kind is taking place back stage in the props department. Custard tarts designed for throwing, not eating, are being topped with shaving foam.

Toad's purple car and Ratty's river boat are both in dock. Roger Redfarn cracks a bottle over a stage hand's head to see if it breaks on cue. It doesn't. "I think you are using too much glue," he suggests. Tries again, only harder. Success. One "concussed" stage hand and one "broken" bottle.

Lunchtime and the theatre bars and buttery are doing good business. In the auditorium Andrew Gardner is still plotting the lights. He sits at the lighting desk with an array of diagrams and a mounting pile of empty coffee cups.

At the lighting console Chris Watts—who has experienced every conceivable pun on his highly appropriate surname—types the lighting plot onto a memory disc. He started at 8 p.m. the previous night and worked until 7 a.m. Then he took a three-hour break before starting another marathon that will last until 11 p.m.

Mid-afternoon: Several streets away at the Ballard Centre choreographer Michelle Hardy is making the cast wish they had taken up a sedentary career like banking. In a hall beyond the splashes and yelps emitting from the fluoride-scented swimming pool the chorus are repeating the movements of the finale so many times you wonder if the needle is stuck.

Michelle, svelte and exuding energy, gees them up, admonishes the out-of-step and cajoles the flagging. Patrick Cargill paces the floor smoking and adjusting his cravat. Terry Scott puffs his cheeks out like a petulant schoolboy. Completing the quartet of comics seeking any opportunity to relieve the exhaustion with a little mischief are Donald Hewlett and Melvyn Hayes.

The chorus is shaping up nicely. Michelle wears a pink leotard with a T-shirt emblazoned with "I'm only the choreographer—I don't count". But no-one is misled by that. She is sergeant major on this parade ground and that's official.

Back in the Theatre Royal the wardrobe department is one step ahead of Wind In the Willows and preparing costumes for the Mother Goose Christmas panto.

Bill Butler, head of wardrobe, is at his sewing machine stitching a prototype hat for the chorus line. "There will be 145 costumes for the panto, without Danny La Rue who has about 17 changes of dress. Once he has left the stage he won't come back on with the same frock."

The principal actors have joined the band in the board room. It is the first time they have sung the songs to full accompaniment. Terry Scott breaks into his Toad's song. Roger Redfarn appears at the door and peers in at the cramped gathering. "Isn't this glamorous. The music, the magic . . ." he quips, and disappears again.

At the stage door Keith is sharing a packet of biscuits with an actor's dog that he has offered to baby-sit for a while. A workman from the council's parks department has called to pick up several shrubs that were loaned as props for a previous performance.

The main actors have now joined Roger Redfarn for rehearsals in the main auditorium. The director is snapping his fingers impatiently. "Come on, quickly. We'll have to run that again. Lights. Right lovies, let's get it right this time!"

A barge woman is supposed to pour boiling water into a bowl. But instead of bubbling over the brim the dry ice leaks out of the bottom. Props dash to the rescue.

"One of the problems in theatre is you can only learn so much because every show is different. What is lovely about Wind In The Willows is it is so wonderfully innocent. It's sad but the world has lost its innocence—it didn't used to be quite so violent and sordid as it is now," reflects Roger during this interlude.

By the end of the evening everyone felt they had done a week's work in the course of a day. But that's showbiz. And, despite, the deadlines and difficulties, no one would have it any other way.

Roger Malone

The place names of Cornwall

Everyone is surely aware that it is by Tre, Pol and Pen that you will know all Cornishmen. And yet, in a way, that is not quite right. Tre, for instance, means a homestead; Pol, a pool; and Pen is a head.

So those famous prefixes are really place names, and it is Cornish place names that have been occupying the attention of one man for the last 12 years, and will continue to do so for at least another decade and probably longer.

He is Mr. Oliver Padel, a Research Fellow at Trevenson House, home of the Institute of Cornish Studies on the campus of Cornwall College that lies in the shadow of Carn Brea.

For all that time—but, of course, it has only been part of his work—he has been involved in a massive survey of Cornish place names.

And that does not mean just cataloguing those quaint names of little villages that the tourist cannot pronounce and wonder what on earth they mean as they drive through the Duchy on their way to cosy holiday-cottages more likely to be called things like Seaspray or the Captain's Cabin.

No, Mr. Padel, a 36-year-old Londoner, has a much wider horizon to his work.

His survey of place names is concerned not only with towns, villages, and hamlets, but names of fields and farms, of wells, of clifftops, and even rocks.

To get an idea of the magnitude of the task, just consider that there are about 200 parishes in Cornwall, and say they each have 1,000 fields. That is 20,000 potential names for a start.

In fact it is virtually impossible to quantify how many Cornish place names there are, but it could well be 500,000.

As Mr. Padel explained, though, Cornwall is a lot more complicated than other English counties.

Obviously that is partly because of the Cornish language—minor names like fields and coastlines are very important because of that language—and another reason is that most English counties have masses of comparative material.

Then there are the different spellings to the names in different languages—in Cornish and English, of course, but Latin and French as well.

Take Marazion for example. It simply means "little market" in Cornish.

But long ago there were two places close to each other and those eventually merged into the one Marazion.

The other was a place called Market Jew and the meaning of that is "Thursday Market". So you find it recorded in French as "petit Marche" and in Latin as "Parvo Foro". But the earliest name for that splendid little seaside village from which so many travel to St. Michael's Mount, is the Cornish one of Marghasbigan.

One publication to emerge from all this research is already in proof form, and the book should come out next year. It is a dictionary of Cornish words and place names—essentially the words, about 500 of them, that are used to make up place names.

Derek Lean

Youngsters go to sea

Hundreds of youngsters between 15 and 21 will sail from Plymouth this year for their first taste of life at sea in the Ocean Youth Club ketch, Falmouth Packet.

They will come from a complete cross-section of society. Some will be shy, some will be extrovert. Most will be nervous, certainly if they have never sailed before.

But in the tight-knit community of the yacht, where the heads provide the only privacy, what will matter is the contribution they are prepared to make to the safe, efficient running of the boat.

Falmouth Packet's skipper, David Crawford, firmly believes the 12 young men and women in the crew should regard the boat as "theirs".

He and two experienced mates are on hand to prevent any disastrous mistakes, but the crew are encouraged to make decisions and carry them out.

"On the first day they come on board they begin to realise it is up to them to get it together and mould themselves into a team, with help from adults, so they can handle the domestic side of things, the social side of things in harmony, and safely sail this boat," said David.

"We teach them all sorts of things, from cooking spaghetti bolognaise to reefing the mainsail in a Force Six off Ushant."

There is only one winch on board the 72ft. boat, which was designed deliberately to be worked by a team. David said four 12-year-olds are quite capable of getting the big mainsail up, provided they work as a unit.

"The principle applies to every activity on board," he said. "Provided they work as a team everything works well. There is room for some individual 'stardom', but it is working together in a group in a 'prison'.

"There is no escape. In a boat you have to get it together. There is nowhere else to go.

"They are a complete cross-section," said David. "A complete social mix. It works 99 times out of 100. I have had only one youngster out of 800 in two years leave of his own accord."

Geoffrey Underwood

Why work?

A young woman of twenty who receives £50 a week after all deductions and free meals for a five-day week has just handed in her notice with the explanation that she will be better off not working.

I hope I do not do the Department of Health and Social Security an injustice but the girl claims she will get more money from them than she does from her employers, friends of mine who run a restaurant.

She has a furnished flat and says that once she is unemployed the department will pay the rent and on top of this she will get a cash allowance.

"Why should I work? I'd rather spend the time with my boyfriend," she told them.

The girl works as an assistant chef and is—or was—splendid at her job. She was trained at a Devon catering college, at the taxpayer's expense, of course, so that expenditure goes to waste, too.

One of my friends told me: "I think it is disgraceful."

John Theobald

The Devons come home

High above the marble quire screen in Exeter Cathedral, trumpeters, in scarlet tunics and white helmets sounded the traditional notes of "Last post".

In the following silence, men in two tiny chapels solemnly turned pages in red-bound roll of honour books—and for a while 300 years history were remembered.

This was only one of the ceremonies that took place in Exeter on Saturday—a day of pomp and pride, circumstance and ceremonial, and of royalty and regimentation.

Because this weekend saw the big commemorative parade, and the symbolic laying-up of regimental colours of the Devonshire and Dorset Regiment in the county capital on celebrating the 300th anniversary of the formation of the regiment.

And what a day it was for spectacle and colour—even if the rain poured down as a representative company of the regiment headed the parade that marched through Exeter city centre and on past the Guildhall where the Colonel-in-Chief of the regiment, the Duke of Kent, took the salute.

There were the crimsons of the 1st Battalion's band and drums; of the robes of the civic leaders; and of the uniforms of the three Chelsea Pensioners who braved the bitter wind and rain and proudly joined the march past.

There were the white aprons of the assault pioneers who spearheaded the parade with their gleaming silver axes—a reminder of those days when the pioneers had to clear the way for the battalion as it advanced.

There was the khaki of the soldiers, led by 120 men of A company, exercising their right, granted in the charter conferring on the regiment the freedom of the city, to march through the streets with bayonets fixed, drums beating and colours flying.

That company as the colonel of the regiment, Maj.- Gen. Colin Shortis explained, was a "working" outfit, having, with a two-week break, come from Ballykinler and two years of operations in Northern Ireland.

Behind them was a guard made up of recruits, juniors and training staff.

And then came the veterans, some bowler-hatted and carrying rolled umbrellas, some wearing their proud red berets, symbolising their airborne connection of the past, and others bare-headed.

But they all ignored the rain and marched with a swagger and style past thousands of clapping spectators who had turned out to pay tribute to the "local" regiment.

They marched to tunes like "Widecombe Fair" and swung their heads in salute as they passed the dais outside the Guildhall where the Duke stood in royal acknowledgement of this special day for the regiment.

The Devonshire Regiment was formed in 1685, originally as the Duke of Beaufort's musketeers to oppose the Monmouth rebellion. With the amalgamation of regiments in 1958 it became the Devonshire and Dorset Regiment.

"It has been happy amalgamation," said Gen. Shortis, "and there is no sense of change or pause."

After the service in the cathedral, the Duke met serving and past members of the regiment, including members of the various old comrades associations, to complete a day which, in the words of Gen. Shortis, had been the regiment's past, present and future marching before its Colonel-in-Chief.

Derek Lean

A Sermon for Mothering Sunday

Mothering Sunday tomorrow is a festival derived from the custom of mother-worship in ancient Greece. Formal mother-worship, with ceremonies to Rhea the Great Mother of the Gods were performed on the Ides of March throughout Asia Minor. With the coming of Christianity this developed into worship of Mother Church, the celebration on mid-Lent Sunday.

Grandmothers are also mothers and perhaps exemplify even more effectively the qualities we look for in mothers. An essay by an eight-year-old demonstrates the characteristics children most value. "A grandmother is a lady who has no children of her own, so she likes other people's little girls and boys. They don't have to do anything but be there.

"Everybody should have one because grandmothers are the only grown-ups who have time."

This is surely rather sad, because what this eight-year-old is really saying is that parents tend not to give their children the time they need and deserve. It is easy to find a hundred and one reasons why this must be, but the fact remains that our young need all the time and care and attention we can spare.

It might be profitable to determine how many young people today find themselves in court because their parents didn't have time for them.

The wise person tries to make time for what is important. It is instructive to study the life on earth of our Lord Jesus Christ and to discover that whatever the circumstances, however tired or hard-pressed He was, He always had time for young and old alike.

Preb J. F. W. Watson,
Vicar of St. Andrew's, Plymouth

Plympton Best

A new beer, specially brewed to suit the Westcountry palate, is now being marketed by Halls Brewery.

Plympton Best, a traditional cask-conditioned bitter with an original gravity of 1039, is the first new beer to come from Halls' mini brewery in Valley Road, Plympton.

The brew is described as a full, malty beer with a well-balanced bitterness and a full, rich colour. It has a smooth taste and is easy on the palate.

Plympton's brewery process uses only traditional methods and ingredients.

Big Day in the farming year

About this time of year—the precise date was something of a movable feast—I used to rise at 5.30 a.m. and board the early morning diesel slowcoach with Paddington as my destination.

My real journey's end was that imposing pile in Whitehall Place where we agricultural journalists gathered for the great set-piece of the year—the annual Price Review.

In many ways it was reminiscent of an old boys' reunion. Scottish journalists, some of them in the kilt and rough tweeds, would greet old friends who had migrated to Fleet Street. And, in turn, Fleet Street's agricultural gurus would extend the somewhat limp urbanised hand of friendship to their colleagues from the sticks. I was one of those.

"How's Devon?" they would ask with a faint note of condescension in their voices. Some of them in their exquisite gents' city suitings unquestionably expected there to be slurry on my soles.

I used to emerge from Charing Cross Underground about 10.30. From there it was a short and quite pleasant walk to Whitehall and Terry Dawes. Terry was the Ministry of Agriculture's Press Officer.

Having passed the vigilantes who lurked in the Min of Ag's impressive vestibule, I would usher myself into Terry's office, there to sup a glass of very good sherry and receive with solemn warnings the "advance copy". Journalists attending the annual price review

Press Conference were divided sheep and goat fashion. There were those members of the Guild of Agricultural Journalists who, like myself, received an advance copy of the Price Review, and there was the common herd of Fleet Street predators and poor unfortunate souls from Poultry World, for instance, who were politely but firmly left with no inkling of what was to come.

The reason for all this secrecy was evident. We were given the advance copy at about 11 a.m. The actual Price Review details were announced in the House of Commons at about 3 p.m. Anyone desirous of earning a fast buck only had to whisper a few vital price movements in the ear of a City gent to earn himself more in five minutes than he received in a year's pay-packets.

So Terry had to be quite sure of the integrity of his chosen few. Moreover, I was confronted by a hard day's graft. Probably the Minister would not finish speaking until 4 p.m. and I had 2,000 or more words to write and phone to Plymouth by 5.30. Phoning a mass of copy like this, with innumerable figures and percentages, can be exhausting. But most important of all, I had the 5.30 from Paddington as my target.

So having grovelled a little to Terry Dawes and conveyed my humble thanks, I would filter through the corridors of the Min of Ag headquarters until I came to the Library. There I would open the hallowed pages of my White Paper advance copy and begin to dig out facts and figures that were to be of utmost importance to Westcountry farmers in the 12 months ahead.

Pocket calculators were unknown, but after poring through various tables and statistics I usually had a pretty good idea of the Westcountry's agricultural fate by lunchtime. Then I could afford to wait with some degree of relaxation for the Minister to arrive. All I needed to complete my two-column story, written in the Chinese version of Pitman's shorthand, were the comments, excuses and perhaps a modicum of self-praise from the great man himself.

But at about 4.15 it would be all over, and I would make a dive for the Ministry's Press telephones, of which there were far too few.

The situation has not changed all that much. When we had our home-grown annual Price Review it was the Minister who took a bashing. Today it is those wicked Common Market Ministers.

Jim Butcher

Having a go at 91

Brixham's battling heroine, 91-year-old Mrs. Lily Hitchcock, gave two intruders "a darn good thrashing" with a walking stick when she realised they were bogus Water Board men invading her home.

Now she is to get a police award for her brave action.

The Good Citizen Award has been made by the Chief Constable of Devon and Cornwall Mr. Donald Elliott, who will present the framed citation to Mrs. Hitchcock at Brixham police station.

A police escort will be laid on for the have-a-go widow, who will be taking along the same trusty walking stick she used to set about the two men, one of whom she even made turn out his pockets before she allowed him off the premises.

Police hailed Mrs. Hitchcock as a heroine when she foiled the raid on her home by the two men in the early afternoon of January 3.

But they warned other elderly people at the time not to emulate the brave old lady because of the possibility of reprisal.

Irene Leonard

Offensive teeshirts

I am not much in favour of censorship but those teeshirts on our streets that plug cocaine infuriate me.

How can people be so stupid as to promote or sympathise in any way with any illegal drug when they must know of the murderous and squalid world of the drugpushers and the human tragedies they bring?

Heroin smuggling has reached epidemic proportions, the Commons was told, and Robin Maxwell-Hyslop, the Tiverton MP, accused the Government of complacency.

It would be interesting to know the quantity of drugs that are smuggled through the Westcountry. We have an enormous coastline and an undermanned Customs service. It still makes some enormous hauls but leaves you wondering how much else gets through.

I am told that there is one airport in the South-West where it is simplicity itself to fly in and out virtually unnoticed.

John Theobald

Plymouth farewell to Marine Band

The curtain came down on 200 years of military band history at Plymouth Theatre Royal on Saturday when the Band of the Royal Marines (Commando Forces) gave the second of its two farewell public concerts before disbandment.

But it was not a night of tears but one of pride and affection from a city proud of its Marines and band.

Emotion came at the end of Auld Lang Syne but the memory of the band lingers on in the hope, expressed both by Mr. Charles Chapman, chairman of Plymouth Music Trust, and the band's director of music, Captain John Ware, that it was a halting point but not the end of band history at Stonehouse Barracks.

The programme included the ceremony of beating retreat, band repertoire favourites and those popular numbers which also place it firmly in the music of the present.

Plymouth Lord Mayor and Lady Mayoress, Mr. and Mrs. Peter Whitfeld led the packed theatre in its appreciation.

Other special guests included Miss Janet Fookes, MP, Major General John St J. Grey (Headquarters, Royal Marines, Plymouth) and representatives of the civil and military life of the city.

"I feel it is a very sad occasion after 200 years," said Mr. Whitfeld. Like many in the audience, the Lord Mayor is a Plymothian who grew up with fond memories of childhood visits to hear the Stonehouse band play.

Special guests included Mrs. Pauline Mathews and Mrs. Sheila J. Hoyte, daughter of Major Frederick Ricketts, director from 1930 to 1944, and famed also as the march composer Kenneth J. Alford.

Two former directors, Captain Dick Stoner and Captain Bert Farlow, were also there for the farewells.

Capt. Stoner, 83, had driven from his West Sussex home to attend. He brought with him a programme of a band concert of 1868, presented to him as a memento by Major Ricketts.

In the best military tradition there was a stiff upper lip response to the disbandment from Capt. Stoner, a director who admitted that "if you are infected with perfectionism then I had a double dose".

A band has gone but Capt. Ware reminded the audience that the Flag Officer's Band remains—at Torpoint.

Robert Earl

Earth closets still

A shock housing survey in West Devon has revealed that a large number of homes lack basic amenities. Many have inadequate water supplies, no baths and some have no drainage at all.

West Devon Council's Health Committee heard yesterday that some houses still have earth lavatories.

Mr. Howard Jones, the council's assistant director, said he found it "incredible that these were still in use.

"Another surprising fact is that 25 per cent of the properties surveyed lacked hot and cold water to a bath and there were well over 100 lacking a bath," he said.

Some houses also had no indoor lavatory, washhand basin or hot and cold water to a sink.

The figures may only be superficial because less than 500 houses with a rateable value of under £75 have been checked so far.

Health officials still have to look at a further 615 in the same rates bracket.

Argyle: so near to Wembley

The Argyle dream of soccer glory ended in the paradox of tears and national acclaim on the lush turf of Villa Park on Saturday. Exhorted and willed to the first FA Cup Wembley appearance by a Third Division team from 24,000 Westcountry fans, Plymouth's players wept emotionally as they were brushed unconvincingly out of the semi-finals by lone goal Watford.

Argyle fought vainly but gloriously to pull back that 13th-minute flash of inspiration from 6ft 4in. striker George Reilly and the universal verdict of Watford's supporters at the end was: "They were so unlucky".

The plaudits were none so fulsome as from Watford's brilliant international winger John Barnes, who won them the game: "We expected them to come out with a flourish . . . but we never expected it to last throughout the game".

The day began with such high hopes. It even looked like fate was on the side of the underdog.

Jimmy Greaves had predicted on television that Watford would win—he had tipped against Argyle unsuccessfully in all the previous rounds. Others echoed the doom.

Buoyant at learning that the Greaves "curse" had been put on the First Division side, the convoy of coaches carrying Argyle's faithful sped northwards. Spirits were raised higher as the route took them past West Bromwich Albion's ground—scene of the marvellous triumph in the fifth round of this year's historic Cup run.

A sense of impending doom only descended when the Birmingham police—with an unfortunate touch of irony—decided to shepherd all the coaches together and it meant that all gathered outside the gates of a cemetery.

But all such gloomy thoughts rapidly disappeared when the teams came out on the pitch. Argyle appeared to a tumultuous welcome.

So Reilly scored and a plucky Plymouth did its best to fight back. When it began to look as if the greenshirts would need some help, the armada engaged in a mass experiment in psychic powers and tried to will Kevin Hodge's last gasp shot into the net.

It did not work—the ball skirted a post.

So the Cup dream ended. But at least Argyle had reached the semi-finals for the first time in its 80-year history.

Western Morning News reporters

SUMMER

The perfect pasty

Our columnist John Theobald has recently been bemoaning that item of food which used to be given the all-embracing title of a "shop pasty". He is right, of course. Some mighty peculiar concoctions have indeed been dreamed up and promoted to the elevated rank of a Cornish pasty. Most do not deserve to wear the uniform, let alone the insignia.

For the true lover of the Duchy's most famous tasty treat there is only one answer—marry a Cornish girl and eat home-made. If she has been well brought up—and being Cornish that will almost certainly go without saying—she will have about as much difficulty in making a good pasty as a dolphin has in swimming. It will be inbred, something learned at her mother's apron-strings, an art handed down from one generation to the other.

She will be able to dice potato as slickly as a gambler shuffles a pack of cards; she will crimp pastry with the dexterity of a concert pianist idly tinkling out a tune on the public bar piano.

There will be no need for kitchen scales and recipe books—the migrating swallow does not need a compass and map. Intuitively she will peel the right proportion of potato and swede, chop the skirt, and slice the onions. Instinctively her pastry mix will be right, not too heavy, but man enough to do the job.

The result, after about an hour's cooking, will be a meal fit for a Cornishman, be he king or peasant.

For a man with a modest appetite the finished product should be a foot long and five inches across at the widest point, piping hot, as nourishing as nature and smelling as tasty as temptation.

The wife, of course, fitting to the more delicate nature of her sex, will have made for herself a somewhat smaller offering, and used the remaining ingredients to make a spare. This is in case, after such a

High above the Tamar Estuary, just above the bridge, a maintenance man cleans salt off the glass dish insulators. Heavy salt deposits from the winter gales were causing short circuits and power failures.
Photo: John Chapman

Falmouth lifeboat "Elizabeth Ann" during service to French trawler "St. Simeon".
Photo: David Brenchley

French sailors after being landed from the Falmouth lifeboat "Elizabeth Ann" following their rescue in extremely bad weather.

gentle repast, her husband should feel a mite peckish later in the evening.

She will, despite the natural aptitude she possesses for pasty making—a sort of culinary heritage—have continually to keep her hand in.

That will be no hardship because, being Cornish, she will naturally appreciate that the other important thing about a pasty is that it is a meal for all seasons, a dish for all kinds of occasions.

A pasty is a lovely lunch, a delicious dinner, or a succulent supper, and, if there is a bit left over there is nothing really wrong with a quick bite for breakfast. Mind you, there is a secret to this, and it is a tip that families might bear in mind.

I remember as a boy—and the first recalled milk-tooth taste for a Cornish child is likely to be that of a pasty—looking at the chunks of cold pasties left lurking on a wire tray in the kitchen, and wondering if the biggest was mine. There was a simple system in our household to save squabbles—one's initials were carved into the pastry before baking.

The other thing about a pasty is that it truly is a moveable feast. It is so marvellously portable, and the Cornish have made full use of that advantage for donkeys' years.

There was nothing like a pasty on a Saturday night, after a bleak and bitter afternoon on the wing, when you prayed the ball would not be worked on the blind side of a five yard scrum because your fingers were too numb to avoid the knock-on. The prospect of a hot bath, a warm fire, and a pasty, deliciously savoury, salt and peppered, and perhaps a little sauced, was part of the week-end's pleasures.

It was as much Saturday's scene as stopping the roar of London's mighty traffic for whoever was in town tonight, or the rich voice of Jim Brady introducing Sport in the West so you knew how "Bonzo" Johns had fared for Redruth, or if Harry Oliver had scored for St. Ives.

In summer, too, it played its part, sliced cold and maybe decorated with a sprig of parsley, laid out on trestle tables in cricket pavilions, a super snack after a warm afternoon in the field. In Granchester it might have been honey for tea, but the chances were that at ten to three in Truro the peckish would have been nibbling a piece of pasty.

For some of us, those with a sense of gastronomic tradition, it is still the rule today. Maybe it is roast beef on a Sunday, or cottage pie on a Monday, but Saturday is definitely pasty day. Not those pocket-sized mince beef and potato apologies that pose as pasties in shop windows, but the proper thing—a handsome thing.

Derek Lean

Cool welcome for county police

Exactly a century ago [3 December 1984] county constables took over the policing of Totnes, but in the ancient borough the change, which should have been routine, sparked off fierce opposition from gangs of protesters.

Mobs roamed the historic streets and angry objectors intimidated local supporters of the county police, according to records in the possession of a Totnes woman.

Mrs. Irene Sollars is the great-grand-daughter of Sergeant Philip Nott, the first sergeant appointed to Totnes by the county. Former Mayor and district councillor Mr. Philip Heale is another of the sergeant's great-grand-children.

The intriguing episode came to light following recent publicity given to the Babbacombe murder 100 years ago.

Sgt. Philip Nott was the brother of Sgt. John Nott, who went down in history as the man who arrested John "Babbacombe" Lee—the man they couldn't hang.

But it was Philip who had to deal with the displeasure of one section of the Totnes community, who resented the county taking over the local police function.

The changeover from borough officers to county representatives occurred at midnight. An eye-witness tells us "at about 11 o'clock the town first showed signs of unusual animation for that hour of the night. Small bands of men paraded the streets and men and women converged here and there, apparently waiting for something to turn up. By 12 o'clock the mob had increased to some two or three hundred and appearances seemed to indicate that had the county police put in an appearance they would have met with a warm reception".

The eye-witness continues: "Starting from the top of High Street the mob paraded the main streets to Bridgetown, many of them being provided with tin pots and other utensils and at some times shouting vigorously."

The noise and uproar was apparently "hideous". "Halting outside the houses of two or three prominent supporters of the county police, the mob indulged in groans and other indications of their disapproval of their policy.

"At the house of one gentleman several panes of glass were broken in the windows and greenhouse."

But the mob knew who their friends were. "At the residence of Mr. E. Windeatt, who had opposed the introduction of the county police, very favourable demonstrations were made, but as it is stated that very considerable damage was done to Mr. Windeatt's flower beds, it is possible that the gentleman may be by this time of the opinion that he would gladly have foregone the honour thrust upon him."

Between about 1 a.m. and 2 a.m., the large crowd dispersed, but not before singing Auld Lang Syne and ringing a few door bells to keep the "peacefully disposed burgesses from sleep".

Sue Morgan

The artists of Lamorna

One might suppose that life in a little Cornish seaside village would represent a world far removed from associations with the celebrated and famous.

Yet, five miles west of Penzance lies the Lamorna Valley, a harboured inlet of picturesque attraction which over the years has had more than its share of connections with renowned figures, from Munnings to the Mitfords, from Augustus John to Robert Newton.

Not surprisingly, many of Lamorna's more distinguished residents have been artists and here one cannot ignore the influence of the nearby Newlyn colony, which originated in the 1880s. When one of its members, Stanhope Forbes, went on to initiate the Newlyn School of Art, Lamorna became a favourite haunt for many of its pupils. A communal flower loft in the woods provided a facility for working in the most inclement of weathers and, from such humble beginnings, some reputations were made.

Alfred Munnings, later knighted, was among those who used the location and the populace to advantage. Developing a special talent for rural scenes and particularly horses, he employed local residents to hold the brldles of his equine subjects while he sketched. I am assured that payment rates were of sufficient generosity to ensure that there was no shortage of willing helpers.

Augustus John was another to provide an occasional extra income for some of the locals. Primarily a portrait painter who, during his career, captured on canvas the likenesses of Lloyd George, T. E. Lawrence, and George Bernard Shaw, he probably had fewer problems with his better-known sitters than with some of Lamorna's aspiring models, one of whom is said to have been particularly scathing in his opinion of an early John portrait. The artist, at first resentful, later bought the man an ounce of tobacco for his "honest criticism".

Yet, perhaps the man who most aptly symbolised the fascination engendered by this quiet hamlet was Samuel John Birch, a painter in oils and water-colours who found the area's artistic potential irresistible. He bought a house overlooking the cove, and lived there until his death in 1955, immortalising Lamorna's name by taking it as his own. A Royal Academician with exhibits in most of England's principal galleries, Lamorna Birch used local settings for the majority of his sea-studies and landscapes.

Occasionally, the village's noted visitors arrived in tandem, as with artist Harold Knight and his wife, later Dame Laura. She was to find a particular niche for herself in her depictions of circus life.

Frank Heath was another artist to erect his own house and studio, a home which was later occupied by a man whose fame owed nothing to art, but everything to his own adventurous spirit, Col. Bill Williams. His exploits as "Elephant Bill", related in his book of that name, made him a popular figure back in the 1950s.

Abstract painter Marlow Moss, initially viewed with puzzlement for her unconventionality, achieved an international reputation during her long residence in the village. Spanish artist Mario Armengol often stayed at Boleigh Farm and is remembered as a man whose humour matched his considerable ability. "How could I catch a fish with a piece of dead cow," he once bemoaned on trying unsuccessfully to fish from the rocks. His bait had been a chunk of meat "borrowed" from the farm kitchen.

Authors, too, have made their contribution to life in the area. Arnold Bennett was among those who spent some months at the cove, as did Crosbie Garstin and Mrs. Alfred Sidgewick whose husband had been a colleague of Einstein's.

Even today, within walking distance along the cliff path, Derek Tangye and his wife Jean have made their home. His books, which have related their lives since their arrival, have long since claimed a captive readership. Further away from the cove, the track which leads on to Porthcurno passes the house of thriller writer John Le Carré.

When one thinks of celebrities, film stars naturally come to mind, and Lamorna has the distinction of having been the home of that definitive Long John Silver, Robert Newton, during the early years of his childhood. Bobby Newton was apparently a rumbustious lad who, when gently chided by his mother, would playfully lift her off the ground and invite her to carry out her threats.

More recently, film producer Stanley O'Toole (The Boys from Brazil numbers among his credits) has lived locally during which time he made a film incorporating several of the current residents as extras.

Among the more ostentatious arrivals in the cove's history was presumably that of Marconi, the Italian pioneer of wireless telegraphy. During his numerous calls on Col. Paynter at the nearby Boskenna estate, he would anchor his yacht off the harbour entrance, thus adding a further touch of glamour to his illustrious reputation.

Not for Lamorna the garish popularity of a Newquay but a whispered recognition that this unique combination of leafy woodland, rippling streams, heathered cliffs and blue-green waters has a rare quality for inspiration.

Lamorna Birch testified to that fact with every brush-stroke and it is perhaps in his work that we find the most eloquent explanation of the valley's elusive attraction.

David Prowse

Crackers

A Plymouth pub last week carried a big advertisement in a local paper wishing readers a Happy Christmas and advertising a Christmas lunch complete with crackers, party hats and so on, with a Christmas fancy dress party in the evening.

The occasion—it was on July 18—is now over. But the advertisement gave me a nasty jolt.

Christmas—in the commercial sense—once a year is quite bad enough.

Christmas, again in the commercial sense, twice a year is well down the road leading to insanity.

John Theobald

Tourism must not be taken for granted

Might the day come when Ilfracombe no longer issues a holiday guide, and hotels and boarding houses at Paignton and Penzance are nearly all converted to offices and flats?

It sounds a silly question. But when you take stock of what changes have been happening to people's holiday habits, it could be one of realistic alarm.

To show how totally different the world has become, let me remind you of a statement that seemed originally perceptive at the time it was made by the planning office of Devon County Council in the mid 1950s. Devon, it said reassuringly, had an exceptional bright future as a holiday area since it was attracting mainly the young and the adventurous!

That surely now seems as quaint as the pre-war assurance in Weston-super-Mare's guide book that if it rained at all in summer it was usually at night or in easily-avoided showers by day.

For whoever else the visitors are who keep Devon's hotels and boarding houses ticking over, especially at the beginning and end of the season, they are not the young and adventurous.

For the Blackburn or Burnley office workers in their young 20s, it was indeed once avant-garde to go on holiday in Newquay. Today most of them would regard it as staid as well as rather expensive—though let me add that Newquay has done much more than most

Westcountry resorts to keep abreast of changes and still makes its visitors happy and content.

Ilfracombe's performance is much worse, if only because people who spend 50 weeks a year in a depressed industrial area do not find a depressed seaside resort scintillatingly different. And what has happened at Ilfracombe should be a warning to every Westcountry coastal town.

When I reported on tourism for this paper in the 1950s and 1960s, I constantly warned that some places were off the rails, and Ilfracombe especially so, ending up off the rails indeed in a literal sense. Twice the council passed a protest resolution; once I was given a severe grilling in the council chamber.

Alas, they were wrong, and refused to learn. Because of lack of clear investment purpose (you even had to pay to get onto the best beach and I believe you still do), the season was not lengthening as at other resorts. That would make it hard for the better hotels to hold their own, leave alone provide private bathrooms and generally improve, I warned.

And that could lead to the double-track railway carrying both Western and Southern holiday trains being torn up while the windy single track to Newquay still flourished. Rubbish! How dare you! they shouted.

They shouted again when I warned that tearing down that majestic Victorian complex which ended its life as the Holiday Inn would take away even more of Ilfracombe's purpose. For the one thing Ilfracombe could have done is become famed as a Victorian resort, giving its freedom to John Betjeman. Now that might be a money-spinner.

But not much money will be spun down to the bottom line of the accounts of catering establishments in Ifracombe this season. I do not wish to abuse the town. Despite the hole they have left through ripping out the Holiday Inn, and other misdemeanours, I still love it as a place, though I could not recommend it to my American friends as one to stop at.

My point is simply that what we have taken for granted—that tourism is here for ever however we treat the tourists—can no longer be taken for granted. The competition will increase remorselessly; the resorts have to fight back with greater effort and understanding.

David St John Thomas

"Very strange kinds of beings"

If you thought that criticism of the Cornish by a woman in The Times recently was a bit harsh on the natives, how about this by a Londoner visiting Cornwall in 1775?

"The common people here are very strange kinds of beings—half savage at the best. Many thousands of them live entirely underground, where they burrow and breed like rabbits.

"They are as rough as bears, selfish as swine, obstinate as mules and hard as the native iron."

The countryside is described as unhealthy "always subject to heavy, cloudy, rainy weather," and food consists of potatoes or turnips, or leeks and pepper grass, rolled up in black barley crust and baked under the ashes (do you recognise the Cornish pasty?).

The people think little of their harsh conditions "but seem to be very happy when they can sit down to a furze blaze, wringing their shirts and pouring the mud and water out of their boots".

The description caught my eye in an article on Cornish Mines and Miners by A. K. Hamilton Jenkin in the 1925 edition of the Journal of the Old Cornwall Society, which celebrates its 65th birthday this year, and has been called "a movement to keep the Cornishness of Cornwall."

The Old Cornwall Society was founded in 1920 at St. Ives. As with all new organisations there was much discussion about its name. "Cornish Society" and "Old Cornish Society" were made and rejected. The first because it was felt to be too vague, and did not distinguish their aims from other Associations outside Cornwall. And the second because it might be thought their only interest was in the long-lost Celtic language.

Today there are 3,000 members of 41 Old Cornwall Societies spreading from Bude, Launceston and Saltash down to Mullion, Madron and Mousehole.

Each society meets monthly, when they listen to speakers, read papers and give information to their Recorder, as well as enjoying a social get together. They also make visits to places of special interest, and attend ceremonies like the crying of the neck or the Midsummer Eve bonfires. Federation meetings of all the societies are held twice a year in the spring and autumn.

June Lander

Real bricks

A zany group from Salcombe are making quite a name for themselves as charity fund-raisers. Dubbed the Blue Brick Club, the amount they raise depends on whether each member has a blue Lego brick on his person at any given moment.

If any of the 15 regulars at the Fortescue Arms are caught without a tiny plastic brick, a forfeit has to be paid. So far £170 has been raised through their strange method and it will help to run the Cavitron brain surgery equipment at Freedom Fields Hospital, Plymouth. Running costs for the equipment are high.

On-the-spot demands to "show your brick" can occasionally be hazardous—especially for club member Pete Searle who is a window cleaner. Fumbling through clothing to produce the vital evidence can be a bit dodgy when you are perched precariously on a high ladder.

Sue Morgan

What a dandelion can do

There was a time when every village had its resident herbalist—a woman who had learned from her mother and grandmother before her the medicinal properties of various plants.

This knowledge, that Nature provides her own remedy for almost every ill, has never been lost. It has simply been updated and used in a more sophisticated way by the medical herbalists of today.

One of these is Mr. Simon Mills, who practises at Netherexe, Exeter. After gaining a medical degree at Cambridge University he decided to combine this knowledge with his lifelong interest in botany. He took the four-year training course for medical herbalists at the National College in Kent and is now president of the National Institute of Medical Herbalists, founded last century to uphold the standards of the profession.

Mr. Mills explained that plants are used to help the body to help itself.

Where a doctor will use an antibiotic to kill the germs causing an infection, the herbalist will look deeper, working on the principle that the body's defences need improvement so the germs will no longer have effect.

Consultations with patients involve not only diagnosing the disease but discovering why it occurred in the first place.

"It means some detective work. We ask about a patient's history, lifestyle and personality and look for clues to the problem," said Mr. Mills.

"The great thing about herbs is that they are available for everyone, and we are all for encouraging people to help themselves," he said.

He highly recommends the humble dandelion, whose leaf provides a diuretic and whose root is a marvellous tonic for the liver.

Chamomile reduces tension and excitability and ribwort leaves will soothe a dry cough.

Oats, whether grown in the garden or taken from a packet, are, says Mr. Mills, "quite marvellous" for the nervous system.

Major docks plan for Falmouth

A full hydrographic survey of the River Fal must be carried out before plans for Falmouth's £73-million container port terminal are allowed to proceed, Truro's MP Mr. David Penhaligon has told Ministers.

His demand came in a late-night Commons debate when Labour MPs representing dock constituencies attacked the port project.

Mr. Penhaligon made it clear that he welcomed the plan, because it would create jobs.

But there was "lingering concern" about the effect it would have on wildlife in the Fal estuary, marine life, currents and the silting up of the upper reaches of the river, he said.

Only a major hydrographic survey, costing £300,000, would clear up these doubts.

At present, a "desk" study is being carried out into the container port plan. But this was insufficient, Mr. Penhaligon told Ministers.

With the promoters envisaging a pier stretching one-third of the way across the Carrick Roads from Falmouth towards St. Mawes, this was "a massive development."

It was the biggest single planning proposal in Cornwall in his lifetime and possibly the largest ever seen in the Duchy. It needed extremely sensitive treatment.

Yet the 1971 Falmouth Container Terminal Act pre-empted normal planning procedures, and meant there would be no public inquiry, Mr. Penhaligon said.

The Commons was discussing the Government's decision to scrap Section 9 of the 1964 Harbours Act, which means port developers can now go ahead with schemes without Ministerial permission. Falmouth is the first of these.

Labour MPs were incensed. Mr. Robert Parry (Liverpool Riverside) accused Mr. Nicholas Ridley, the Transport Secretary, of behaving like Pontius Pilate. "He is washing his hands of all responsibility."

Attacking the Falmouth scheme, Mr. Parry added that there was massive over-capacity. "The docks industry needs another container terminal like a hole in the head."

Mr. Eddie Loyden (Liverpool Garston) claimed that Falmouth was being used to undermine the National Dock Labour Board scheme, of which Mr. Ridley had been a vociferous opponent in the past.

Mr. David Mitchell, Parliamentary Secretary for Transport, told them that their fears were unjustified.

"We are facing cut-throat competition in world markets," he said. The scrapping of Section 9 was to enable British ports to compete successfully.

Turning to Falmouth, Mr. Mitchell said the promoters envisaged most of the traffic being transhipped into smaller ships. Only a small proportion would be off-loaded for rail and road transport.

Falmouth Container Terminal Ltd., was willing to pay for any improvements to the Truro-Falmouth branch railway line which were necessary, he said.

"However the traffic goes it will be good news for the future of the railways in Cornwall."

On road links, however, Mr. Mitchell made it clear that the Government would not expect to pay for any road improvements arising from construction of the terminal.

He did not reply to the Truro MP's point about a major hydrographic survey.

Persistent starling

A chirpy new resident has made his mark on villagers at Harbertonford. The newcomer, a sociable starling, moved in with the country community a couple of months ago and his reluctance to leave has prompted mixed feelings.

Since he took up residence, the speckled bird has developed a liking for children, cars and homemade cake. Each day he can be found with youngsters gathered in the village centre to await the school bus.

When they return from school he is there to greet them.

Hopping from head to head and hand to hand, the friendly bird has become part of the village scene—to the consternation of one or two aggrieved residents.

The owner of a local store is less than charmed by his preference for human company. When shoppers file into the store each morning to pick up their daily newspapers, they are often accompanied by the persistent newcomer who has been known to cause chaos to the well-ordered business.

On one occasion, after skimming several times over the well-stocked shelves, his beady eye alighted on a favourite food and within seconds he had plunged his beak greedily into a pile of meringues.

And when the feathered fiend opts for a change of scenery, he hitches a lift inside any convenient car—causing mild panic among the occupants.

Sue Morgan

The marina "disease"

The "marina disease" is spreading westwards, threatening our estuaries and upsetting the lives of local people.

Plymouth, which already has its fair share of marinas—Sutton Harbour and the Mayflower, to name but two—is now in a quarantine period for yet another.

Marinas are all very well in their place—out of sight or providing shelter in an otherwise exposed area, such as Torquay—but people appear to have a misguided regard for them. Whatever you call them, they are no more than floating caravan sites.

I feel sorry for the residents of the Barbican and Coxside who, if the planned marina in the Cattewater goes ahead, are going to have to wake up every morning to a mass of glass fibre parked uninvited on their doorsteps. Dream boats belonging to people who live miles away will become their nightmare.

This marina will completely alter the character of the Barbican. Boats will no longer be seen swinging independently to the rhythm of the tides and winds as they have done for centuries. Instead the ugly face of commercialism will confront the onlooker who will find it hard to distinguish one boat from another.

The developers say the marina is designed to cater for the large events in the yachting calendar besides offering permanent and visiting berths. But who is catering for the locals? Why should they be deprived of their birthright and denied free access to the sea?

For some months now, charges have been enforced for launching boats—even small dinghies—where once there was no cost.

The man with an open boat and a few pots to tend will soon become a character of the past. How can he possibly afford the extortionate prices of a marina?

Besides the cost of the marina, there are other nasty side effects. More untreated sewage going directly into the Sound. Schools, who use the area for training youngsters how to sail, will be forced into the main shipping channels and the channel into Sutton Harbour will be severely restricted.

These are known problems. No one can tell what effect the marina will have on silting if it goes ahead.

Is it fair that part of the Cattewater in Plymouth should be turned into a rich man's playground?

Jenny Killingbeck

Cornish police

A police force in Cornwall was "uncalled for, unnecessary and un-English" in the view of the parishioners of Veryan in 1857.

The inhabitants of Lanivet thought the same, and a petition

was sent to the House of Commons asking for the repeal of the Police Act.

Despite these protests—thought to be because it would bring heavy additional rates—a county force was set up of 179 men, consisting of one chief constable, 17 superintendents and inspectors and 161 men (to include a sergeant major, 16 sergeants, 48 first-class constables and 96 second-class).

Today the combined force of the Devon and Cornwall Constabulary is nearly 3,000, and because, since amalgamation, relics of the force are getting difficult to find, Mr. Ken Searle, the Police Historian for Cornwall, who retired from the force last year and is now a funeral director at Pool, near Redruth, is keen to add to the collection he started five years ago.

This includes examples of the different types of helmets issued to the borough and county forces; tunics, belts, badges and buttons, whistles, oil lamps, old photographs, cutlasses and truncheons.

A decorated truncheon, with a clip to attach it to a belt, which belonged to a member of Truro City Police, is thought to be the only one in existence.

Books in Ken's collection include the Rules and Regulations for the guidance of the Cornwall Constabulary, printed in 1900 and inscribed "The Sergeant at Truro".

It has 157 pages of closely-worded instructions for policemen, with an index starting at "Accoutrements, when to be given up"; through "Jealousy, to be avoided"; "Lamp, properly trimmed"; "Overcrowding steamers" and "Prize fights" to "Whistle, to be taken on beat duty".

Constables were exhorted to use their intelligence and discretion; keep their temper, not associate with bad characters, never to be seen carrying an umbrella or stick when in uniform, or to smoke on duty, and not to frequent public houses or taprooms, whether on duty or not.

On entering the force he had to provide himself with a decent suit of plain clothes, two pairs of high-low boots, one pair of black knitted gloves, four shirts, six pairs of stockings and a notebook and pencil.

Another early book called "Self Education for the Police" belonged to Walter W. Wright, PC66 of St. Ives.

It includes handwriting and arithmetic tests, as well as sample reports on such things as "Removal of a lunatic," "Searching box of servant," "Open-air preaching," "Fare refused in tram car" and "Age of person deemed incapable of crime".

Policemen worked seven days a week, nine hours a day, with only a week's leave.

Many constables walked between 30 and 40 miles a day, although they could travel by train at reduced cost.

Superintendents could use a horse and carriage, but travel rules were strictly enforced and one constable was dismissed in 1861 for riding in his donkey cart, and another for getting a lift in a miller's cart.

In 1898 bicycles were allowed on duty, but only in cases of emergency—crime, sudden death, fire or serious accidents—and their use had to be entered in red ink in their weekly journal. These were kept by officers up to the grade of superintendent, until the practice ceased in 1957.

By 1904 seven offences had been recorded under the Motor Car Act of 1903, but it was not until 1920 that members of the force were allowed to use their own motor-cycles—again only in emergencies. They could then claim 3d. a mile, and 5d. for a combination.

Following the Road Traffic Act of 1930, mobile police were introduced, and in 1931 six Sunbeam Lion motor-cycles were purchased, with four years later six Austin Eton 11.9 open two-seater cars.

In 1946 a Traffic Department was set up, and today there are 97 vehicles in the Mobile Policing Division, motor-cycles and an helicopter, with a total fleet of over 600, including vans and commercial vehicles. Men wishing to use bicycles can do so, but, I gather, there aren't many around.

Clashes between police and miners are nothing new. In 1873 when two miners were tried at Camborne for assaulting the police, 500 miners, armed with pikes, stationed themselves on the road outside the town, determined to rescue the prisoners.

The chief constable arranged for them to be spirited out of the court by a back door, while he went to Truro to meet the prisoners who were to be put on a train for Bodmin.

Meanwhile, the superintendent and his men from Camborne had been driven out of the town, and an inspector struck down by a stone. Troops and extra police were called in, and the riot resulted in injuries to four constables and damage to the police station, town hall and two public houses.

The case against the rioters was proved, but the chief constable, Col. Gilbert, came to the town hall to hear complaints against the handling of the riot by the police.

He conducted the inquiry in "a thoroughly impartial spirit, which appeared to give great satisfaction to the public".

The first chief constable was Col. Walter Raleigh Gilbert. One of his ancestors was Sir Humphry Gilbert, the discoverer of Gilbert's Straits, and a half brother of Sir Walter Raleigh.

He was chief constable for nearly 40 years—one of his last duties being to cope with the Newlyn fish riot of 1896.

A crowd of a thousand had gathered on the pier at Newlyn, tempers having risen to boiling point because the Newlyn men would not fish on a Sunday, while the visiting men from Lowestoft did.

After they had sent the crews of a dozen East Coast boats ashore, they threw the whole of their catch, amounting to 100,000 mackerel, into the sea.

Fishermen from Porthleven, Mousehole and St. Ives arrived in support. A strong contingent of police came in, followed by 300–400 men of the 2nd Berkshire Regiment by train, reinforced by a torpedo destroyer from Plymouth, with three more posted in Mount's Bay.

After fighting in the streets, when several people were seriously injured, the authorities persuaded the Lowestoft men to man their boats and leave the port.

The incident took its toll of Col. Gilbert, who had been directing operations at the age of 83. He became ill a few days later, and died within six months.

June Lander

No privacy under the sea

The nuclear-powered submarines of the Second Submarine Squadron move dark and menacing in and out of their base at Devonport to spend long periods deep in the oceans.

The Duchess of Kent talking to children during her visit to R.A.F. St. Mawgan in February 1985.
Photo: John Chapman

Chelsea pensioners march past the Duke of Kent during the tercentenary parade of the Devons and Dorsets in Exeter.
Photo: Mike Uttley

Pilchards being landed from the "Silver Harvester" at Newlyn.
Photo: Andrew Besley

To the layman watching them slide quietly past Devil's Point at the mouth of the River Tamar, they are mysterious, perhaps evil-looking.

But for the ships' companies living cheek by jowl for weeks on end, these formidable fighting ships are home, work-place and a source of great pride.

Captain John Round-Turner, who commands the squadron, has seven nuclear-powered but conventionally-armed submarines running from Devonport. Five are Swiftsure-class boats and the other two are HMS Trafalgar and HMS Turbulent, the first of the Trafalgar-class.

He is also responsible for three nuclear-powered boats and two conventional submarines in refit and for the administration of submarines building at Barrow-in-Furness. He has 1,850 all-ranks under command, just over 1,000 of them in seven running submarines.

"My primary task is to ensure the submarines in the squadron meet the tasks imposed and the standards set by the Flag Officer Submarines," said Captain Round-Turner.

"We get the boats to sea in a proper material state and a properly-trained state. At sea, they are under the operational control of the Flag Officer Submarines. We look after their interests and their people as sort of long-stop and forward planning organisation.

"The South Atlantic is a continuing commitment for boats from the squadron," said Captain Round-Turner. "They make operational training patrols throughout the Nato area of interest to gain experience of the sort of environment they may operate in war.

"There are two or three trips a year to the Western Atlantic where we undertake trials in the Atlantic Underwater Test Evaluation Centre in the Bahamas."

The squadron makes tactical deployments, carries out trials of new equipment and undertakes surveillance on the likely "opposition" in war.

Much of a running cycle is likely to be spent at sea, submerged, with the ship's company working a six-hours on, six off watch routine.

Captain Round-Turner said not all submariners are volunteers, but the majority of those "pressed" into the service decide they want to stay.

"They like the life, the comradeship of a close-knit community and the extra pay they get," he said.

Space is at a premium and lack of privacy is something the submariners must accept. Even the tiny curtained space of a bunk may not be a sailor's own domain. It is not uncommon for up to 40 per cent of the men on opposite watches to have to share a bunk.

"Hygiene is there, food is there and there are all sorts of things to occupy you off watch, but the one thing you have not got is privacy," said Captain Round-Turner.

"They are a super bunch of people. There is nothing quite like them."

Geoffrey Underwood

Water shortage–whose fault?

As every Westcountryman knows, the briefest spell of sunshine brings with it the threat of water restrictions—drought produces a crisis. We live in one of the wettest parts of Britain. Is it too much to expect that adequate provision is made to store the rainfall in winter to tide us over even the driest of summers?

An anatomy of the Westcountry water story reveals a horrifying epic failure: a star of ill-omen has hung over all attempts to resolve the shortages. Finally, the weather itself has mercilessly exposed man's failure. Emptying reservoirs and faltering river flows spell out the indifference of Nature to the Westcountry plight.

But just who is to blame? Is it Lady Sayer, and her determined and effective band of Dartmoor preservationists. Could it be that she alone has stemmed the construction of reservoirs on the Moor against the might of successive governments?

A large majority of Westcountry people genuinely believe this to be the case. Are they correct?

But what of the others involved in this sorry saga.

Why, for example, did then Enrivonment Secretary Michael Heseltine dither for four years over a decision on the Roadford reservoir? And why did his predecessor, Peter Walker, shuffle the water authorities around at a time when demands were outstripping reliable supplies?

What induced a Parliamentary Committee of four MPs to throw

out the Swincombe reservoir proposal only halfway through the hearing? And can any blame be attached to the former local-authority-dominated area water boards who, during the 1960s, sought to build what are now seen as pitifully small and inadequate reservoirs of parochial proportions?

There have been 20 years of time wasting, two disastrous decades of delay. And not until the end of the 1980s can there be any guarantee of uninterrupted supply for more than 800,000 water consumers for huge areas of North, Mid and South West Devon and the city of Plymouth.

Vast quantities of water still run daily to waste in Plymouth, while its citizens are implored to save. That, despite the fact that in 1980–81 alone, South West Water spent £681,000 on waste-detection. The distribution system is old beyond belief, but until the Government of the day allows the water authority to raise the cash to remedy the defects, millions of gallons of treated water will continue to run to waste.

Great blunders are often made, like large ropes, of a multitude of fibres. To unravel the strands in this particular rope, it is necessary to go back to the 1960s.

Then, water supplies in Devon and Cornwall were controlled by eight small, and often fiercely independent water boards and two river authorities, one for each county; there were also no fewer than 72 sewage disposal authorities.

On Dartmoor, a bitter battle of words was being conducted between the North Devon Water Board—which wanted to construct a reservoir at Meldon, inside the National Park—and the preservationist lobby led in uncompromising fashion by Lady Sayer.

Plymouth, also running out of reliable supply sources, turned its attention to Lee Mill, nine miles east of the city: it would have been a cheap source, but with little or no room for expansion after the end of the century.

South West Devon Water Board, whose customers lived in the Torbay area, was also in the hunt for more water.

Plymouth and South West Devon joined forces and proposed to build—with the blessing of the national body, the Water Resources Board,—a huge reservoir at Swincombe, on Dartmoor, a saucer-shaped, lonely expanse of moorland at the heart of the National Park.

To the water board's utter astonishment, a committee of four MPs—John Hunt, John Cordle, George Wallace and Michael Cocks without, as far as is known, even visiting the site—totally rejected the Bill after a 17-day Parliamentary hearing which cost its promoters about £300,000.

Amazingly, the honourable gentlemen heard only one side of the argument—that advanced by the promoters of the Bill themselves—before throwing it out. Even the objectors could scarcely believe their victory was so complete.

Plymouth and South West Devon licked their wounds. Could their presentation of the Swincombe case have been really that bad, they wondered?

The Cornwall River Authority had, meantime, been doing homework. They came up with a site for Plymouth at Lamelgate, in Jamaica Inn country, from which a 19½-mile long pipeline would feed water to the city. Cornish nationalists were outraged, there was a threat to blow up any such pipe.

What about Bickleigh valley, outside Plymouth, suggested Cornwall. A storm of local opposition promptly greeted that announcement, and even the Devon River Authority thought there were better schemes to be considered.

Both river authorities now presented their Section 14 Surveys—a summary of ideas to provide water for the South-West up to the year 2001.

The list of threatened valleys was, by now, endless—and, wherever a reservoir was planned, protest instantly mushroomed. Need I remind you of schemes for Townleigh, Huccaby, Hill Bridge, Notter Bridge, Ward Bridge, Foxworthy, Lovers Leap, Scribble Downs et al, et al.

If there was rage and confusion locally, Parliament itself had its own ideas of sorting out the water scenario. Enter Peter Walker.

Appointed by Ted Heath as Minister of the Environment, Mr. Walker quickly decided to sweep away all the little water boards, the river authorities and the tiresome sewage councils. Instead, his Ministry for Living proposed to regionalise the whole outfit and create ten authorities who would be charged with managing water from the skies to the tap and beyond.

The water industry itself, knowing the cards were about to be shuffled, almost ground to a halt. Not surprisingly, officials began to jockey for positions on the new authorities for jobs with previously undreamt of salaries.

The promotion of desperately needed new reservoir schemes took a back seat, as Walker's radical reorganisation took almost four years to implement fully. It was a delay which regions like the Westcountry could ill afford.

It is true that Meldon was finished and opened, that the Upper Tamar Lake scheme got off the ground, that Wimbleball, on Exmoor to serve Somerset and East Devon was agreed upon. But a scheme for Cornwall (eventually to be at Colliford, on Bodmin Moor) and for Plymouth remained in abeyance.

But South West Water, led by the controversial figure of Major George Gawthorn, got quickly into its stride. By 1975, Gawthorn, and his team of experts, had persuaded the authority members to adopt a regional strategy of large reservoirs—at Wimbleball, Colliford and Roadford.

Had all gone according to plan, all three reservoirs would have been in operation by 1982 or 1983 at the latest. There need have been no drought restrictions last summer or this. But Gawthorn's hopes were never realised.

South West Water was plagued with worries—Westcountry MPs were infuriated by the seeming high-handed attitude of the new authority—and over the horizon, unknown to us all, crept a natural phenomenon, predictable but wholly unexpected—a once in 250 year drought.

It shattered the authority asunder. Major Gawthorn, now a sick man, retired from the scene, his Colliford scheme still to be approved, his Roadford project still as far away as ever.

By 1978, the authority was ready to face the considerable agricultural opposition to its scheme to drown hundreds of acres of good land at Roadford, on the Devon-Cornwall border, near Broadwoodwidger, to serve the 800,000 threatened consumers in Plymouth, South West and North Devon. Sir Peter Mills, MP, led the agricultural opposition alongside such district authorities as West Devon and Torridge. "Go back to Swincombe" was the cry, but the Water Authority would not budge. A Swincombe reservoir they pointed out could hardly serve North Devon.

What, however, becomes entirely inexplicable and consequently inexcusable, is the fact that the Department of the Environment, under Mr. Michael Heseltine (a former MP for Tavistock) sat on the results of the public inquiry into Roadford for two years.

Heseltine, when finally his department did respond, suggested that a site at Higher Hordlett, near Holsworthy, should be examined.

Another year was wasted, and then another until Mr. Heseltine almost grudgingly conceded—four years after his inspector had recommended it—that Roadford could be built. Even then Heseltine's men would not approve plans for the full-size reservoir which will in any event be needed early next century.

By the beginning of the autumn [1984] a start will be made at Roadford. But while Wimbleball protects Exeter and East Devon, and Colliford (from next year) protects Cornwall, for 800,000 consumers there can be no guarantee of protection of supplies until Roadford is finally built, and that will be 1989, since reservoirs cannot be constructed overnight.

Is then, Lady Sayer, the person whom we love to blame for inadequate water resources, really responsible?

Two people who are in an excellent position to judge, Major George Gawthorn, past chairman of South West Water and Mr. Len Hill, the present chairman, will have none of it.

"Definitely not," said Mr. Hill, who for seven years now has been dealing with the Department of the Environment.

What are we to blame then? Procrastination more than personalities? A disgraceful lack of overall planning rather than individuals? Politics more than protesters?

There is another factor, and one which weighs heavily in this whole vexed question. I well recall Sir William Goode, chairman of the Water Resources Board, gazing out across the Swincombe saucer 16 years ago: "The real problem," he audibly muttered for the Press's benefit, "is that there are far too many possibilities".

The die has now been cast, the decision made. Surely the Water Authority should now be left to get on with the task at all speed, with the support of people and politicians.

James Mildren

Fresh fruit, please

There is little evidence of a higher incidence of scurvy in the Westcountry than in London or the rest of southern England, but I would not mind betting that the intake of vitamins is considerably lower here. Despite this being the region that produces much of it, we are still not particularly fresh fruit and vegetable orientated at table.

Much though I prefer living in the South-West, one of the more appealing aspects of London is its fresh produce—and competitive prices. As I spent a busy day dashing round the Capital, I looked closely at the displays of fruit and vegetables (and flowers), both in regular shops and on street barrows. The average is well above what you see in the South-West.

Of course, we have some excellent greengrocers. Generally, local shops do not bother to display their wares so well or so lovingly though. The produce is not as fresh, also it tends to be more expensive.

Indeed, the latter point comes as no surprise. Often I have been told by people moving from London to the West that they are delighted at saving money in many ways, especially on transport and eating out, but that food shopping is generally more expensive, greengrocery especially so.

I remember how things were when I was fruit farming in South Devon in the late 50s and early 60s. Almost any day in the strawberry season I could have bought the fruit retail from barrows in London's streets and sold it profitably wholesale to local shops. Yes, I do mean that. The price that South Devon shops paid me was higher than retailers were asking in London. By the time the local shops had put their margin on, the differential was usually more than a half.

Of course, I did not complain at the time. What businessman does complain that he is being paid too much? Moreover, I grew my strawberries not only with technical skill but great love. They were the best in the world, I claimed, and, perhaps, worth a higher price.

That rationalisation did not work. For, in addition to the best variety, I grew the pink turnip one that is pretty tasteless but looks passable even when you maltreat it or the weather upsets things. And I got the same high price for them! Everybody in South Devon just presumes that strawberries would be expensive.

Cornwall, incidentally, is even worse than Devon. The intake of vitamins seems to decrease as you go west, with Newquay as an especially black area. The prices charged for not especially fresh fruit and vegetables there in high summer has always been stunning—though Scotland's Western Isles and resorts on Ireland's west coast put vitamins at an even greater premium.

Nor is it just the average private individual and family who seem to buy less really fresh produce in the South-West. Comparable hotels, boarding houses and all kinds of institutions like hospitals do so too, I believe. Fresh fish you may get, the meat will undoubtedly be better, but the runner beans will have hung around for days before any remaining vestige of freshness is cooked out of them, and strawberries in or out of season treated like caviar, though, of course, generously drowned in cream.

I also used to grow beans, which because of their bulk I sold to a wholesaler. It was bad enough that he did not expect a daily picking and delivery, but regularly he passed onto shops beans he had stocked for a week. The shops did not mind.

Every town has shops displaying cauliflowers and sprouts so defunct that they should have been put out of their misery in a compost bin days before.

But I have not a clue what we can do about it.

David St John Thomas

The ha'penny back in Cornwall

A tourist attraction has taken delivery of 10,000 freshly minted halfpennies—the first Cornish coin to be produced for over 170 years. They are the first batch in a total order of 400,000 for Halfpenny Park at Wendron near Helston.

The design chosen for the new coin is an exact copy of that used on the last Cornish penny in 1811. It shows an engine house with a horse whim on the obverse and on the reverse is a pilchard lying between four ingots of copper and three blocks of tin.

Mr. Peter Young, boss of Halfpenny Park, which includes Wendron Forge and Poldark Mine, was faced with a difficult decision when the Government decided to do away with the ha'penny.

"I had spent £60,000 publicising the new facilities here under the heading of Halfpenny Park, with an admission price set at a halfpence.

"I was appalled at the Government's decision. It undermined the whole basis of the park, where the total investment then approached £1-million."

Mr. Young's first reaction was to fight the Government and try to prevent it withdrawing the coin from circulation.

But after taking expert legal advice, he wrote to the Chancellor and asked for the ha'penny to be left as legal tender so that he could buy enough coins to last him for several years.

The request was refused but then local MP David Mudd stepped in and took up his case with the Treasury. The compromise reached was that Mr. Young could have his own coins minted and use them as legal tender within Halfpenny Park.

So the entrance charge is still a half-pence. Everyone who hands over a penny receives one of the new halfpenny coins as change.

They can be spent inside the park, but Mr. Young expects almost all of them to be kept as souvenirs.

"They are quite beautiful and we don't expect to get many back. They will go all over the world as souvenirs."

Cornish coins were in circulation for centuries, though the most famous was the last to be produced. The 1811 copper penny was issued at Scorrier House, near Redruth, for use in the mining districts.

David Green

Messier than seagulls

There is, I hope, little chance of anyone taking seriously a request by a resident at Ilfracombe that the resort's seagulls should be culled because they create havoc in their search for food.

Of course seagulls will scatter litter and tear open plastic garbage bags and make a lot of noise.

But they will never make as much mess and create as much noise as people do and whereas there is a solution to the problems created by seagulls, no one has come up with a solution to those caused by humans.

Tougher bags and gull-proof litter bins are both available. But nothing is available that will prevent vandalism such as is caused by louts who enjoy kicking garbage bags around until they spill, and upending litter bins.

Going to live in or visit a seaside town and then complaining that the seagulls are a noise nuisance is rather like going to live in the countryside and complaining that pigs smell and cows leave droppings on the nice green grass.

The day that seagulls start flying around playing transistor radios will be the day to start talking about culling them.

John Theobald

Hard work and a happier life

Judith Cook is a good writer, experienced journalist and Shakespeare scholar, who has come from Stratford to live in Cornwall. I think she has adopted us, for one half of her new book *Close To The Earth. Living Social History in the British Isles* (Routledge and Kegan Paul, £9.95) is about the famous old Cornish industries, and the way people worked and lived. It makes a lovely book, with speaking illustrations of our old folk and places, sailing ships and harbours, tin mines and the fellows going up and down in the skip, haymaking and harvest home.

The other half of her book is about slate quarrying in Wales and making those coracles—in which I fancy the early Cornish saints came across the Bristol Channel; iron mining in Warwickshire, fishing from Lowestoft. But I am fascinated by what she tells us about our own people. She has had the good idea of getting some of the older generation to give us their stories.

Some of them remember getting a hard living by tin streaming. Quite authentic: the father of a schoolfriend of mine kept his family by tin streaming from the detritus of the rich lodes around Polgooth, at St. Austell. Then the days of fishing fleets—I can remember how beautiful the lights of Mevagissey boats looked in our bay on a summer night! A good catch, and pilchards would be hawked around the village, sometimes a dozen for a penny.

"From Christmas to February," says a Mousehole fisherman, "we fished off Plymouth's Bigbury Bay banks, and they never failed". Then "furriners" invaded our shores, and we have a fine account of the Great Newlyn Fishing Battle of 1896 against them. Sorry to say, the Penzance men joined with Lowestoft against Newlyn—now what about Cornwall's motto: "One and All".

We are given an illuminating account of oyster fishing in the Fal—I had no idea how odd and idiosyncratic it was. Quite right: "Oysters is a mystery," says an oyster man.

Most moving is the account of the tin miners and the hardships they went through—climbing those ladders, bad air and the workings under the sea; early deaths—and the Levant Mine disaster of 1919, when the beam engine failed and 31 men crashed to their death.

Village life—no sanitation or indoor water, no electric light or washing machines: I remember it all. I lose all patience with young people today, for ever protesting about this and that, when everything is done for them. We were brought up hard—and are the better for it. I hate softies. A Scilly Islander says: "One wouldn't wish the hard times back from the past, but it was a better place."

Several of the old folk say that, and that people were happier. Why?—because they worked. Judith Cook tells us how. She has a good chapter on Dartmoor; next time I hope she will explore further into beautiful Devon, up to Exmoor and even into Somerset and Dorset!

A. L. Rowse

"A parish priest by trade"

The new Bishop of Exeter is to be the Right Reverend Hewlett Thompson, who has been Area Bishop of Willesden, London, since 1974. He said yesterday that at the age of 55 and having been a bishop for 11 years he had been wondering where he would be going next. "Exeter was a wonderful surprise."

Bishop Thompson will succeed the Right Reverend Eric Mercer, who retires at the end of May. Before going to Willesden, the bishop worked entirely in the parish ministry. He was a curate at Northampton, Vicar of St. Augustine, Wisbech, and Vicar of St. Saviour, Folkestone.

Because of that parish background, he sees his role as bishop largely as "enabling the parishes to do their work".

He was named after his godfather, the late Dr. Hewlett Johnson, the "Red" Dean of Canterbury, who was a friend of his grandfather, Canon Lewis Donaldson, a noted Christian socialist.

The fact that the Red Dean had been his godfather must not be taken as an indication of where he stood himself, but he was very proud of what his grandfather and godfather had done in their day.

He thought that there were different vocations among the episcopate. Some church leaders had a genuine calling to engage in public issues and were bound to be seen sometimes to be getting close to party political lines.

"But that is only one line of vocation. There are other lines. I am a parish priest by trade and so my particular work, both in my present job and, as I see it, maybe in my next one, is to enable the parishes to do their work."

By that he meant animating, "feeding" and assisting the parishes in conveying the Christian gospel in the conditions of today.

"I am essentially a man of the middle—which doesn't mean sitting on the fence but holding the various emphases of the Church of England together."

Peter Vince

The last Cornishwoman in Helford

Other people dream of, save for, and plan towards holidays abroad each year. They long to sample life in a different country and atmosphere and feel that is the only way they can dodge the pressures of everyday working life.

But my idea of heaven is to drive further down into Cornwall, stay in a cottage and go each day to find out more of my home county; to renew old acquaintances with long-loved places or to discover parts of Cornwall I have never had the chance to explore.

This year I went with an old friend who, like me, has always been in love with Cornwall. We rented a cottage in Helford village.

I had never before appreciated the experience of living right in the centre of a village like Helford where the cottages hug the steep banks that lead up from the inlet of the river, where boats are parked outside doors like cars elsewhere, and where voices waft out of windows and from terraces, verandahs and doorsteps. I was reminded again and again of Dylan Thomas's Under Milk Wood.

Each evening we sat on our doorstep in the slanting golden sun and watched and listened to this protected world go by. Not many Cornish voices, for Helford is a holiday village, but one people treat with respect.

There was nothing ruinous about the tourist presence. French, German and varied English accents were the sounds we heard. The holiday mood was infectious, unwanted pressures had been left at the top of the hill. In Helford worry appears to be banned. The sense of limbo is complete.

We had no telephone, the television hardly worked, twice when we turned it on the news looked like flashed signals from outer space, bearing absolutely no relation to our lives. It was hard to believe that strikes and fights and picket lines and spies and politicians were anything at all to do with our world of water, trees, birds, boats, sand between the toes and pink sunsets on gleaming river waters.

In holidaytime Helford the place is full to overflowing. In the winter it is a different thing. There is only one Cornish woman still living there and she will be gone by the winter.

Emmie Hewett was born in Helford at the beautiful thatched cottage of Rosemullion. She was one of twelve children and she remembers her childhood as a supremely happy one. Her father was a farm labourer at Kestle Farm and her mother took in laundry to help supplement the meagre income. Times were often hard.

"In those days," Emmie told me, "we were all working class people living in Helford. Now there are very few people who live here through the year, maybe five or six full-time residents. You couldn't wish for nicer people but it's not like having your own. It is a gloomy place come winter though you wouldn't believe it now."

Emmie married her husband, Frank, just after the war and moved into Rose Cottage where they have lived ever since. They have built onto the cottage and 30 years ago Emmie started her famous cream teas. Now thousands of people have sat in her perfectly-tended terraced garden looking up river at bobbing boats and swooping birds, eating Emmie's delicious home-baked cakes and scones and splits.

But now the hills and slopes are taking their toll. Emmie's arthritis is beginning to worry her and come October she and her husband will move to Mannacan, over the brow of the hill. She will be next to the cricket ground and the church and four of her sisters.

Helford still holds its own, retains its somehow hallowed atmosphere. Ten minutes walk away from the centre of the village you can be on the banks of Frenchman's Creek and feel the mystery and excitement that took charge of Daphne du Maurier's imagination and led to her famous novel of that name.

When I went last week there was no-one there. Perfect silence, with the sun shining on the mud flats. A heron sat midstream, then flew down the creek to fish in the shallows. And sharp and clear and mournful the curlew cried. For a moment the world was idyllic, so beautiful it hurt. And that's what a Cornish holiday is all about.

Sarah Foot

AUTUMN

Schoolhouse on the Moor

Prehistoric stone circles and medieval mineworkings are not the only signs of man's past activities on Dartmoor. There is a continuing legacy of decaying cottages, deserted farms, and worked-out quarries.

Just beyond the track leading up to North Hessary Tor with its television mast, on the left as you go towards Tavistock is another path leading to Yellowmeade Farm.

Walking beyond the farm, you soon realise you are following granite sleepers, now largely overgrown, that formed the track carrying trucks of stone from Swell Tor quarry just ahead.

Here are the ruins of the quarrymen's cottages, and larger buildings that perhaps were engine-houses. The quarry itself is now a tranquil lake, surrounded by sheer walls.

Away in the distance you can see the sea shimmering near Plymouth. The moor lies calm and still about you, but this does nothing to dispel the air of melancholy which always seems to me to pervade these areas where man has once been active and now is no more.

Returning to the road, and again going towards Tavistock, you soon find a car park on the left. It is an unusual car park—just a flat space on open moorland, but distinguished by an E-shape of dry-stone walling surmounted by weather-beaten beech trees.

Many visitors to this car park wonder what the walls represent. They are in fact all that is left of Foggintor School, built in 1913.

"The school in the middle of nowhere" they called it—and with some justification, as it was roughly two miles from each of the hamlets it served, Rundlestone, Swell Tor and Merrivale, in the heart of Dartmoor.

Standing on a bleak, exposed site, facing north, it sometimes took the combined strengths of the headmaster and the visiting attendance officer, one on each side of the door, to get it open, such was the force of the wind.

In 1895 the Foggintor member of the recently-formed Walkhampton Parish Council complained that there were 60 small children in that area receiving no education at all, and suggested the Mission Hall (demolished in 1965) be used as a school. The hall trustees agreed, and charged £5 per annum for its use.

Under the 1902 Education Act a board of managers was established, responsible to the newly-formed County Education Authority. But the building was considered unsuitable for a school, and the legality of its use was questioned so Foggintor School with a master's house was built. It closed in 1936 owing to the closure of all the quarries except Merrivale, and transport to Princetown School (founded 1862) was provided.

Lionel Govier, of Whitchurch, was headmaster of Walkhampton School for 30 years. He says that Foggintor had only one headmaster, F. S. Stoyle, in the whole of its existence.

Mr. Govier gives some interesting detail about an even older school in the Swell Tor area, provided by the quarry owners. The census of 1861 gives a population of 267. The school had a headmaster aged 69, and a schoolmistress aged 15!

To this school went at least one who achieved fame—Henry Edward Duke, born 1856, journalist, M.P., lawyer, judge, president of Probate, Divorce and Admiralty Division of the High Court. He was created a baron in 1925, and took the title of Baron Merrivale of Walkhampton.

He died in 1939. One sister was Mrs. Bolt, who with her children Louie, Greta, Wesley, Dingley and Ewart, ran that comprehensive village store in Princetown known as "Bolt's".

The doorway was festooned with boots and shoes. On the left as you entered was a long counter stacked with bales of materials and boxes of cottons.

To the right was the grocery department, where you could buy anything from potatoes to biscuits. Miss Louie presided over this, and beyond was the domain of her brother Ewart the butcher.

Each area had its own special smell. In a little box at the far corner, suspended it seemed from the ceiling, sat Miss Greta, dealing with the cash which travelled to and fro by one of those miniature overhead railways so fascinating to a child.

I can even remember some of the things my mother bought there for me—a white straw hat trimmed with rosebuds, a pretty cotton dress for our first holiday at Teignmouth. And we never left the shop without Miss Louie giving me a sweet or an apple.

Mr. Rooke, now of Gunnislake, was a pupil at Foggintor from 1916 to 1924.

"It was a happy school," he says, "with 70 pupils. The teachers were wonderful, and all the subjects were taught, including gardening for the boys and needlework for the girls. There were two classes with cloakrooms and the floors were of blockwood."

Mr. Les Brown, now of St. Breward, also went to the school. He says that if their fathers were rich enough, the children took vacuum flasks to school. Otherwise they had bottles of cold tea.

Pasties were heated and clothing dried on the hot pipes which provided the central heating.

The school team had their own coloured jerseys but no pitch. They played "on the moor" against other schools such as Princetown.

Little used now except by tourists in the height of summer, the site is lonely and windswept.

But it is easy to imagine the lively scene 50 and more years ago when groups of children could be seen coming to school from several directions.

Barbara Stevens

The rigours of redundancy

At the start of the third week since redundancy I feel a hint that I am being persecuted. Nobody is advertising a job that suits me; no one replies to my numerous letters. The post is awaited anxiously; the columns of the newspapers are searched; the JobCentre is visited as part of the daily ritual to find out what is new.

Then the first refusal arrives: "Thank you for your interest . . . large number of applications . . . applicants who have more relevant experience than your own . . . etc."—well at least I got a reply. Then the telephone rings: a trip to Bristol for an interview. I have to pay for the trip. It may come to nothing.

It's years since I was last interviewed; am I up to it? I have got to be. I must be positive in selling myself and my talents. The day arrives and, yes, I am nervous; isn't that human? I am anxious to please, and the pressure is on me. Clean shirt, polished shoes, the mind continues to rehearse without the voice saying a word.

I arrive exactly on time, and my arrival is announced by the telephone. Next comes the statutory wait with just a hint of a cold sweat. Just be yourself I have been told. Five minutes becomes seven and I wait for the tension to ease. I am announced and introduced and receive a warm welcome. The brain is working faster than the voice. "Never open your mouth until your brain is in gear"; I slow down and the nervousness lifts. The interviewer shows interest in me. We exchange questions searching for common ground. Then comes a stinker of a question: "What are your weaknesses?" The mind races again; this wasn't in the rehearsal. After a long silence here comes my answer: "We are all human and I have weaknesses like any other human being, but the best person to ask is my wife." It may not be the answer, but at least it is my answer.

After an hour the interview is over. How have I done? When shall I start? Have I performed well? All these unspoken questions go unanswered except for a blank expression and "We'll let you know. I am interviewing throughout the week, and you are one of many applicants who are being seen, and then a short list will be created before the final decision is made." I interpret this to mean: "We've got all the time in the world, and so many people want to work for us that we are bound to find somebody suitable, and it is unlikely to be you."

Finding a new job is going to require time, patience and money.

The author is a former managing director.

Parson in the lifeboat crew

Twice in the last two years a Plymouth clergyman has been called from a service to rush to the lifeboat to join in a rescue.

The Reverend Ian Watson, curate of St. George with St. Paul's, Stonehouse, and of St. Andrew's Church in the city centre, is assistant mechanic with the Plymouth lifeboat.

He has held the post for the last two years, but this weekend saw him acting as duty mechanic for the last time. He leaves the crew at the end of this month and will become Vicar of Matchborough, Redditch, in March.

Mr. Watson, who is nicknamed "Boots" because of his years as a Royal Marines officer, is thought to be the only clergyman in the country serving with a lifeboat crew. He believes another clergyman was in a crew about 50 years ago.

He regrets having to leave the crew and said: "The crew are a tremendous bunch of blokes. I shall really miss the fellowship I share with them on and off the boat."

Lifeboat coxswain John Dare and the second coxswain, Pat Marshal, invited Mr. Watson to join the crew and he has been on a good many calls in the last two years.

Last November he was in the lifeboat in a Force 9 gale when it went to assist the coaster Fylrix listing badly off Rame Head. Three ship's crew members were rescued by helicopter and the remaining five were taken off by the lifeboat in the Sound.

On a summer Sunday in 1983 Mr. Watson had to rush to the boathouse in Millbay Docks shortly after the end of morning service. He had no time to change out of his dog-collar. The lifeboat picked up a diver, who was unconscious and suffering from "bends".

"I was giving him first aid in the after cabin when he came to, looked very confused and bemused and lapsed into unconsciousness again. I realised I was wearing my dog collar. He probably wondered where he was," said Mr. Watson.

"On two occasions I have had to leave a service to go to the lifeboat. Once was to go to a yacht on fire off Plymouth, but we were recalled off the Eddystone.

"Last year there was a yacht sinking off Cawsand. My bleeper went off in the middle of prayers at Holy Communion. Preb. John Watson, Vicar of St. Andrew's, continued with the service.

"I disappeared in my robes down the aisle of the church having collected one of the crew, who was in the front row."

He recalled returning from one search mission when the lifeboat was hit by a wave which dropped into the well of the boat and threw it on its side.

"I pray every time we go out," he said. "I would not be telling the truth if I said I was not frightened. I am frightened sometimes, but I think that is a good thing.

"Often we have so much work to do you forget what is worrying you and you get on with the job. It is worse for the families at home waiting and knowing there is a hooligan blowing."

Geoffrey Underwood

Old-fashioned whitewash

Plumbers' tallow, brown sugar, salt and quicklime are a few ingredients which apparently can help to keep your Devon cottage damp proof and sparkling white for many years.

These ingredients help to make up the old-fashioned lime and tallow whitewash which several South Hams residents are now using instead of modern paints.

Mr. Dick Barton, of Harbertonford, is one house owner who swears by the time-honoured method. He says the age-old wash keeps homes fungus free, is about a third cheaper than paint and lasts about three times as long.

His snug stone cottage has recently been treated with the recipe by Totnes builder Mr. Roger Reay, of Smithfields. Mr. Reay does point out though that once treated with lime and tallow modern paints must not be used later, as the wash causes paints to peel.

Sue Morgan

The Bishop who rocks the boat

Theological arguments seldom make news. Or at least they didn't until Professor David Jenkins left his University job last year to become Bishop of Durham.

Some of the things he has been saying have become a kind of man bites dog story. Here is a Bishop who seems to have doubts about the virgin birth and resurrection of Christ, and that's news. Those who know Jenkins well are sure of his sincerity and he has been well known for years as a vigorous talker, always trying to explain Christianity in ways that ordinary people outside the Church can understand. Still, Bishops are meant to steer the boat, not rock it, hence the debate.

Only talk about your certainties, preachers used to be told. If you have doubts, keep them to yourself. But that was long ago, before Television took an interest in Church leaders. Now they are asked to explain the most complicated matters in a few minutes before the camera, and half of what they said is edited out. I sometimes wonder what would have happened to great thinkers like Freud or Einstein if they had to explain themselves to Sir Robin Day in 50 seconds flat, sandwiched between the latest news of the miners' strike, and today's value of the pound.

That said, violent controversy about Christian belief between Bishops and other theologians is no new thing. In the early days, they shouted at each other, pulled each others beards, and walked out when they could not agree over such tricky questions as how Jesus could be called both man and God. It is actually that question which lies beneath the present arguments about how Jesus was born and how he survived death.

If he was simply God dressed in human shape, he could arrive and depart as he wished. If he was just an inspired prophet he could have been conceived by Mary and Joseph in the normal way, and left his body in the grave like other men. The early Christians agonised about these questions, and their answers are in the New Testament and the Creed.

It is easy to have sympathy with those who are alarmed at the present discussions, and would prefer to stick to the old truths. Once settled, no good can come of reviving the old controversies. But there are others, like the Bishop of Durham, who feel that won't quite do. So much has changed in our understanding of the world, and in particular of medical knowledge, that we need to find new ways of expressing old truths. Thus, the resurrection was not merely a conjuring trick with bones (did anyone think it was) but the taking by Jesus of a new form, so that he could be present and known spiritually to all later generations.

Since there are millions of Christians who reckon they are in communion with Christ in their daily lives, is it not sufficient to say that fact is far more important than any kind of description of what went on in a tomb near Jerusalem the first Easter morning? But, comes back the immediate reply, unless he physically rose, there would have been nothing to prove Jesus was alive for evermore, and so no Church at all.

Christians, like everyone else it seems, want to be sure about some things, open minded about others. We need a mixture of certainty and freedom. We want a creed to rely on, and individual liberty of conscience in religious matters, as in everything else. So we find some people who are very firm about the Bible and very flexible about church organisation, others who sit lightly to the Creed, but are appalled at changes in the Prayer Book. It takes all sorts to make a Church.

The Rt. Rev. Peter Coleman
Bishop of Crediton

The bookmaker's burden–and addiction

Ever since on-course bookmakers first laid the odds, punters have long waged battle against "the old enemy" trying to beat the starting price.

Yet visions of bookies walking from the course with their satchels and pockets bulging and lighting their cigars with £10 notes are far from reality.

About 90 per cent of Silver Ring bookmakers for instance have a back-up job or income outside racing for they would not survive on the small courses where turnover is low apart from the lucrative Bank Holiday meetings.

Thirty-seven year old Newton Abbot bookmaker Joey Oliver is pretty typical of the Silver Ring brigade. He has been laying the odds for the past 10 years on his bookies pitch.

"I was interested in racing from an early age and recall going to Buckfastleigh as a real avid jumping fan. I used to admire the old jockeys such as Fred Winter, Tommy Shone and the 'Iron Man' Jack Dowdeswell.

"Years later, when I graduated to the Newton Abbot Grammar School I used to leave early on race days and watch as the likes of Graham Thorner and Bob Davies would drive their tired mounts into the last fence as if it were made of paper," said Joey.

On leaving school he became a police cadet, training at Tiverton. After four months he was offered a trial with Somerset County

Cricket Club and at 17 packed in the police immediately.

Joey reported to Somerset on the Monday, meeting an Australian at the gates, who was also to have a week's trial—none other than Greg Chappell.

He stayed the full week. "I was sent home on the Tuesday. Greg finished up captaining Australia and I ended up skippering the South Devon club," he said.

When his police career ended the Newton Abbot youngster became a bank clerk, hating every minute of the 18 months in the monetary world, and then worked in the fish and chip shop of his father and mother, Jack and Olive, for ten to eleven years.

It gave him the opportunity to continue his love of cricket where he has made his mark as wicket-keeper and batsman and over the past 19 years has played nearly 100 times for Devon.

Unfortunately, because of his bookmaking he missed two of the county's best seasons in the Minor Counties including its championship success in 1979.

"As racing became more and more dominant in my life, I felt bookmaking was the answer, but I didn't really do my homework.

"I was completely naive about the whole system and did not realise until it was too late to stop my licence application that opportunities were so limited," he says.

Joey now covers 19 courses although it has taken a long time to build them up.

While he is by no means moaning and says he loves being involved in the racing scene, he makes no secret of the fact that, while Bank Holiday meetings are lucrative, it is the bread and butter winter meetings where it is at times difficult making ends meet. At a meeting at Leicester in December for instance, he left after three races having taken just £32.

The weather was dreadful, there were 14 bookmakers and about 21 punters and it is not difficult to see there was a loss after paying staff, travelling expenses and other fees.

"In racing, a bookie is only as good as his pitches and I certainly have some bad pitches. Small fry bookies like myself hang on in there waiting for the better pitches, which take years to come. Many of my friends have laughed when I say things are bad and so to prove the point I have taken the disbelievers with me.

"Believe me they have all been amazed by the uneconomics of the job and have all duly apologised. If anybody does not believe me, they are welcome to come racing with me. Bookies carry on because they are addicted to the game and hang on until the next Bank Holiday," said Joey, who added that he believed the layers still gave far better value than the Tote.

He firmly believes that the removal of the 4 per cent on-course betting tax would bring extra crowds to racing and that Sunday racing is a must. The possibility of floodlight racing should be looked into, as well as having more evening fixtures at the end and beginning of the season.

"Racegoers in the Westcountry are really lucky to be able to enjoy such fine facilities as those at Newton Abbot as well as such good up-and-coming jockeys and trainers. The facilities on some of the Midlands tracks are very poor compared to here," he says.

Joey says he has no regrets at being a bookie. "I love the life and the atmosphere and I am convinced that things will get better in the future. In any case I am hooked on the job, whether they do or not."

John Balment

Keeping out the Devil

They stand like well-fed sentinels, watching and waiting at the entrance to the village. Corpulent characters, Falstaffian, rotund in their spread.

And like guards of famous places anywhere, they claim their fair share of public attention. They are not strangers to the camera's lens or the interpretations of the artist's palette.

After all, they could scarcely be called upon to perform a stricter surveillance or more vital vigil. Their mission of security is to guard against the Devil himself.

They are, of course, the round houses at Veryan, that little village nestling in one of the gently undulating valleys of Cornwall's Roseland area.

Built of cob, conical roofs thatched with straw, tiny windows framed by stones, they were built by a man called the Rev. Jeremiah Trist.

There are two stories ascribed to these unusual dwellings, and I know which one I prefer.

The slightly more mundane is that the designer paid a visit to South Africa and was so impressed by the Kaffir kraals that on returning to his native village he built the residences after the style of them.

There were five built, two before you reach The Green coming into the village from the Tregony direction; two up the hill on the narrow road that leads to Carne beach; and one tucked in behind the village school.

Four of them have crosses perched on top of and slap in the centre of their circular roofs but the other one—and its roof is of slate—merely has a chimney pot.

It is said that the cross on the roof is to render the householder and his family immune from evil spirits and that this is an old Cornish custom.

The better story is that Parson Trist was a man who formed a great affection for his little flock and, like the good pastor he was, worried about their well-being.

So he hit on the idea that was not only to give the village a splendid architectural distinction, but one that would well and truly foil the designs of Satan.

The crosses were there to ward off the Devil all right, but, as a belt and braces job, just in case he should come at night and not see the crosses, the houses were built round so that there would be no corner in which he could hide.

I have reason to believe that is true, because more than 40 years ago I lived in one of those round houses—the one called "Beehive"—and in all the time I was there never once did the Devil appear.

Mind you, the village has grown somewhat from the place I knew as a boy. It always had charm and a certain style, but it seems to me more elegant now.

The stone houses and cob cottages have been smartened up and Great Grandmother Channon, whose dress was always as black as her Cornish range, and her hair as white as her apron, would scarcely recognise her home.

The noisiest neighbours in the village of St Veryan are still the raucous rooks wheeling high over the tall beech trees.

The village remains a place of neat cottage gardens, lovingly kept, and even at this time of year—because the Roseland climate is softly temperate—the hydrangeas are still blue with flower, the odd rose rambles, fuschias flourish, and the camelias are in bud alongside the path that leads to the church.

There is no better evidence of the Roseland's balmy climate than the semi-tropical plants that grow in the little garden given to the village by a man called Macleod in memory of his wife Eppie.

She, so an inscription in the garden tells us, "loved flowers and all beautiful things, and her neighbour as herself".

And the garden, which has a small lake and a tiny island, was laid out and presented to the people of Veryan "to be for all time a place of rest for the weary, happiness for children, and of beauty to everyone".

Happily the garden remains, and a fine feature it is.

No, Veryan has not changed that dramatically since as a boy I went to that church where my grandfather, who was nicknamed "Shepherd"—a kindly term for a kindly man—gave forth in his rich baritone voice in the choir.

Those were the days of the war, and when in summer you walked the lanes, with their high hedgerows hung with honeysuckle and framed by foxgloves, to swim at Carne Beach you found it tangled with the scaffolding of anti-invasion defences.

Now the only invasion to be concerned about is the annual one of holidaymakers, so many of whom come to explore and enjoy, and gaze at those lovely round houses with their intriguing legend.

Derek Lean

The Prime Minister as hostess

It's the sort of invitation you can't and don't refuse. Mrs. Thatcher had invited some 50 or 60 editors of regional newspapers with their wives to Downing Street for an hour-long Press conference followed by a reception hosted by Mr. Thatcher and herself. We went, we saw, we were conquered.

The Prime Minister arouses ambivalent emotions, both among her allies and her opponents. She's bossy. She's dictatorial. She cannot tolerate opposition. She always wants to win. She hates compromise. She's heartless about unemployment. She's the Iron Maiden. Those are the usual complaints.

Yet what came over on Monday night—and Mrs. Thatcher was obviously trying to impress—was the softer maiden. She was attentive to her guests and their wives. She moved steadily around the room to make sure that everybody had an opportunity to meet her. She was smiling and cheerful in spite of the day's news of the pound. There was a ready answer to every question, even to how she kept her hair so immaculately groomed. (A wash once a week and curlers every day, if my memory is correct.)

At the Press conference itself, her mastery of a bewildering range of questions was superb.

The issues came at her thick and fast. South West regional aid. North East regional aid. Water Authority secrecy in Yorkshire. The Michelin redundancies in the Potteries. Textile slave labour in Leicester. Stansted. Ulster. Youth unemployment in Liverpool. To each she had answers, often in minute detail.

There was no hint of weariness or any visible toll from her five years of office as Prime Minister. She remains slim, alert, occasionally taking an audible intake of breath briefly to consider her thoughts before answering, occasionally leaning on her elbows when she is going to hammer home an answer of Thatcherite conviction.

Some of the range of impressions left with me were:

> She clearly supports the introduction of water charges instead of water rates.
>
> She remains implacably determined that there will be no more concessions to miners and will see the dispute out, however long it takes.
>
> The passion index rose perceptibly on the subjects of rate-capping and the entrepreneurial spirit—the need for companies to sell service, quality and competitive pricing.
>
> Asked about Tory critics of the Government, she defended its record at length, but used the first person: "What *I spend* on the health service."

Here was a woman and a politician and a Prime Minister at her peak and in her prime, convinced of the rectitude of her policies, determined to push them through, eager to persuade each and every one of us of her rightness.

Agree or disagree with her, in detail or totally, you would need to be up in the morning very early indeed to beat her.

Brian MacArthur

Steady business for the pawnbroker

Perhaps the most extraordinary news item I have come across in the past few days is the report of the opening of a pawnbroker's shop in the thriving cathedral city of Truro.

In fact, the opening of a pawnbroker's shop almost anywhere, with its Dickensian image of poverty and hardship, would bring a raised eyebrow in 1984.

Across the road from my flat hangs a pawnbroker's sign but it remains there as a reminder of another age and it must be many years since the last pawnbroker's shop closed in Plymouth.

A glance at the Yellow Pages for the area shows not one listing. The whole Bristol area has only two.

But there is a gap in the market, apparently, for one jeweller who opened the pawnbroker's shop in Truro reports steady business and hopes to open another at his Redruth premises.

As far as he is concerned pawnbroking is a respectable business offering a service that is needed, and who is to argue with him? We are constantly besought to borrow money from financial concerns of all kinds and this must be the least complicated method of all.

Popping down to uncle's is obviously going to return to fashion. Nonetheless, it still strikes me as an extraordinary development and it will be interesting to see whether pawnbroking re-establishes itself widely.

John Theobald

Read all about it

Times have certainly changed from those dusty-dark days when a visit to the local library seemed to be a silent struggle to find something more exciting than a pre-war Agatha Christie or a biography on someone of whom you had never heard.

Indeed, now when it comes to the business of borrowing books the world is literally your oyster.

You can live in a little Devon village like Chittlehamholt and order a book that will eventually arrive having come from a library in

California. And all it will have cost is the usual reservation fee of just 25p.

These are books—or it could be an article in a particular periodical—required by people who are immersed in research or study of some highly specialised subject, and they have looked to their local library for help.

Mind you, such exotic transactions do not happen all that often. Last year, for example, the Devon Library Service borrowed only 15 books which actually came from libraries abroad—countries like America, Germany, Switzerland and France.

In the other direction just three of the county's books—and there are two and a quarter million of them—were sent across the seas to satisfy people who, for strong personal reasons, wanted to get sight of a certain volume.

The fact is that while most of us look to the library for nothing more demanding than a good read, or to provide books on particular subjects in which we have an interest, a lot of people, engaged in research or study, call on the library service—and it might be the mobile that parks in the village square—to provide some pretty obscure stuff.

Last month, for instance, someone called at Exeter's Central Library wanting a book on old instruments for extracting teeth.

At Plymouth, not so long ago, a person wanted to track down an article on a mechanical banana peeler.

And at Sidmouth someone else wanted to find a book on the mathematical treatment of billiards.

Even with the book stock held by the county they are hardly the sort of subjects you would expect easily to find on the shelves.

Over the years, though, libraries have built-up this reciprocal arrangement of helping each other out, and putting their individual strengths—Devon is rich in its collection of local history and in Plymouth especially it is strong in naval history—at one another's disposal.

In fact there is a South Western Regional Library System which involves ten county library services with between them something like 5,000 public libraries and about 15-million books.

So when someone calls for a book or publication that Devon does not hold it can turn to that organisation for its assistance, and it is all done on a quid-pro-quo arrangement.

In 1983 Devon borrowed 2,043 books from that source, and in return the other libraries in the region borrowed 3,565 of the county's volumes.

That regional organisation is not confined to public libraries, but those of universities and polytechnics, of colleges and Government departments.

Mr. Roy Eden, Devon's Bibliographical Services Librarian, explained that all the libraries pay a subscription to the organisation —the inter-lending is only one of the services it offers—which has a small staff at Bristol and where the office works as a clearing house.

Even with that Aladdin's Cave of books as a resource, it is still not possible to meet everybody's requests.

So there is another system whereby librarians can turn to the British Library Lending Service which has at Boston Spa in Yorkshire, stored on 84 miles of shelving, nearly 2,500,000 books, 172,000 periodicals, all manner of reports, dissertations and conference proceedings to mention just some of the written material in its possession.

It has a staggering 1,395 miles of written matter stored on microfilm, and rather modestly says that one of its objectives is to provide as comprehensive a reference service of last resort as possible. The division works closely with libraries and information centres both in this country and overseas.

Mr. Eden said the stock holding there was called on by libraries throughout the United Kingdom and indeed the world.

In 1983 Devon borrowed 1,553 items from the British Library Lending Division.

When someone visited Newton Abbot library last year wanting a particular book on the butterflies of India—such a book was published in Calcutta—to Boston Spa it went.

I had to chuckle at one of the request forms sent off to the British Library Lending Division recently. The person concerned wanted a copy of "How to be a Happily Married Mistress". That sounds like an interesting piece of research.

Derek Lean

Pub at the end of the world

The old pub stands serene on the edge of the village green, near the tree-shaded church, about half-a-mile from where the Atlantic rolls home bearing white necklaces. The towering cliffs here are furrowed like the face of a Red Indian, the spray paints its own rainbows and, in summer, pale English faces can soon turn berry-brown.

This is Morwenstow, a remote parish tucked away in the north-east corner of Cornwall, and once described by John Betjeman like this: "Here one is reaching not only the end of Cornwall, but, it seems, the end of the world".

The place, though, does have its charms. Walking around this parish, up the hills or through the lovely little wooded valleys, safe from the motoring crowd, one can share with Wordsworth: "The calm existence that is mine when I am worthy of myself".

The Rev. R. S. Hawker was vicar here from 1834–75, and apart from all else he did, eccentric and otherwise, this poetic clergyman ensured his place among Cornish immortals by composing "And Shall Trelawny Die". This is still sung, passionately and appropriately, in pubs throughout Cornwall, and nowhere is it more appropriate than in Morwenstow. Hawker wrote the ballad two miles away in the pretty little hamlet of Combe.

The pub in Morwenstow, the Bush Inn, is one of the oldest in the Far West—a 12th century inn, formerly a chapel. Harvest Festival here has a special significance since it was Robert Stephen Hawker (again!) who first introduced the autumn festival, now celebrated all over the world.

The Bush Inn, looking out over open commonland and the famous church, St. Morwenna, offers a roomy, airy, comfortable bar and St. Austell Best Bitter. Also on draught is a bitter I haven't come across in other hostelries in the county—Devenish (Weymouth) Wessex Best Bitter. Devenish, in fact, was originally a Weymouth brewery established in 1742.

They still love to talk about the past in the pub: the smuggling, the ghosts, the wrecks, the wrecking. And, of course, the redoubtable Hawker.

One local told me that the vicar used to send a villager with a basket to collect the "gobbets" of shipwrecked sailors; bodies of sailors were often buried in the churchyard. I also heard that

Hawker, a practical joker in his youth, was not joking when, at the age of 20 and desperately hard-up, he married his well-off godmother.

And shall Trelawny dine, there is a good choice of food in the Bush Inn, which deservedly attracts many visitors in the summer. There is a pleasant garden for eating and drinking, and the prices do not leave you rattling your small change and wondering where all the folding stuff went.

Roy Bolitho

Del's double, Totnes trader

That street-wise BBC TV series Only Fools and Horses is always a must for one familiar trader at the regular Friday antiques market at Totnes.

The chirpy Cockney proprietor of Dell's Antiques never misses a chance to watch the comedy show whose central character is a "dead ringer" for himself.

And he is convinced that he was the model for the show's fast talking Del Boy played by the versatile David Jason. "It's uncanny—our lives run on a parallel course," he said.

Before moving to Devon he was a familiar face around the London markets, did a "bit of building", had a flat in Peckham and ran a battered old van—just like Del Boy.

His stamping ground was around Woolwich and Sidcup the familiar haunts of Del Boy, grandad and brother Rodney.

Coupled with coincidences like being stitched up over the sale of a family oil painting, the cheerful dealer pointed out that the TV character wears the same distinctive hats, uses the same pubs, and pool rooms and had a stall in Petticoat Lane. "Friends in London ring me and say they've just seen me on the telly," he said.

Why is our Westcountry gold and silver trader so sure? He explained that years ago he was a regular at a snooker hall just off Fleet Street, also used by national newspaper reporters.

He got to know one particular Fleet Street man, who, he says, is now writing for television. "That could be the answer—I got to know him quite well."

Although happy to talk casually about old London haunts and the TV coincidence, he insisted his surname must remain a mystery. "Do us a favour—no names. Know what I mean?"

Sue Morgan

Vintage touring

Of course they did things with a lot of panache and style, those magnificent men in their motoring machines.

In the years of the first decade of the 20th century, in their four and six-seater open tourers like Landaus and Cabriolets, they embarked on the grand tour of the United Kingdom.

It was only 24 years since the invention of the petrol engine, but progress had been rapid, and by 1908 horseless carriages had become quite sophisticated motor cars.

They could certainly travel long distances, and reach speeds of up to 60 and 70 miles per hour.

Even so, motoring was very much a gentleman's pastime, and there were only 40,900 cars on the road compared with today's 15-million.

So quickly, though, were the ranks of motorists growing, that an organisation or club was needed to look after their interests.

Just three years previously one had been formed. It was called the Automobile Association and Motor Union, and it too had a certain style, particularly in its language.

In the first year of the Great War, for example, it proclaimed: "that little brass badge, with its twin A's and its spread wings, is the modern motorist's shield and buckler, his passport and his guide.

"With this talisman on his dashboard he may enter upon the true and full possession of the traveller's birthright—the open road."

Stirring stuff, but that intrepid motorist, travelling along bumpy roads, perhaps at night, with only the beams of his acetylene gas or paraffin lights to show the way, often wanted something more practical than a shield and buckler.

For a start he wanted somewhere decent to stay—and considering that probably half had a chauffeur, he wanted somewhere for the driver to get board and lodgings as well.

So in 1908, three years after the AA came into being, the organisation decided to register hotels, and to recruit the hotel keepers as agents.

The first list of AA appointed hotels was published in the 1909 members handbook and ran to 24 pages, which means that this year the motoring organisation is celebrating 75 years of inspecting hotels.

It was not in fact until 1911 that the then AA secretary, Stenson Cooke, introduced the idea of using stars for hotel classification.

Even so that 1909 members handbook blazed the trail for say, the 1985 one, which is published today and which runs to more than 750 pages.

And today's will include more than 20 hotels in Devon and Cornwall that were originally listed.

75 years ago at one Exeter hotel you could get a bed for 4/6d; lunch for three shillings; dinner for five shillings; and free garaging for AA members.

A single room, with bath or shower, and breakfast in that same hotel today will cost £27; lunch from £5.50; and dinner from £7.50.

Back in 1908 when the AA decided to register hotels there were a number of motives for the move.

As the AA's Archivist, Mr. David Tuckfield, told me: "We decided it was necessary to give members information about hotels which were suitable and agreeable, which would give help and service, and make sure our members got a good reception and treatment.

"We were anxious to advance the feeling that if you were a member of the AA you got something special."

One of the special things was a bulletin board which had a central lockable compartment.

AA members—and there were only about 7,000 of them compared to today's 5,500,000—could open it with a special key to reveal messages of all kinds of road information.

One typically terse piece of advice read: "Road between North Tawton and Okehampton in very bad condition."

That cupboard, though, also gave information about hidden police speed traps.

As Mr. Tuckfield explained, the speed limit 75 years ago was 20 mph and although obviously there were not patrol cars and radar traps, the police were still out to catch the nifty driver.

Then they used three men on such an operation, one in uniform, and two in plain clothes.

They would measure out a furlong and station men at either end equipped with stop watches. If the second man clocked a speeder he would signal to the third officer further along the road who would stop the offender.

Presumably such traps were regarded as not being quite cricket, because the AA were certainly conscious of road safety, and quite often their patrolmen, in khaki tunics, breeches, and black leggings, reported members considered guilty of furious driving, and gave them a ticking off.

A perk to be found in hotels then for AA members was a cabinet containing towels and brushes exclusively for the use of members—a somewhat scathing indictment of the general level of hotel facilities at that time.

So the £2 2s a year members—today basic membership is £24—got quite a lot of service for their money as they journeyed around on petrol costing as little as 1/6d a gallon.

The patrolman for example—and if one did not salute, members were advised to stop and ask why—were even equipped with packets of telegraph forms in case anyone wanted to send a telegram.

They must hve been doughty men because they went on duty at 9 a.m. and did not knock off until it was really dark.

If they noticed anything wrong with a car as it went by they would blow their whistles.

They were able to assist in roadside repairs, but only in cases of emergency, but they all knew how to fix a tyre, and in those days that was the most common mishap, a lot of times stemming from nails thrown from horseshoes.

Derek Lean

The rich flavour of pure-bred beef

Farmers are facing another battle that is assuming gigantic proporions: the crippling constraints being put on producers of beef and of lamb to turn out animals that are in the super lean category, yet capable of passing the grader's scrutiny.

Generations of Westcountry meat producers made their money by sticking to the basic principles of the old music-hall song: "A little of what you fancy does you good." Today's housewife hums a far different tune: "What is convenient is best."

Spaghetti Bolognese, home-made beefburgers, packet burgers for the deep-freeze, frozen cod steaks, fish fingers, incredibly cheap frozen chicken, turkey steaks and a host of other convenience or "fast foods" are at her finger tips. "Chips with everything" is of course today's motto.

That incredibly rich flavour of succulent pure-bred beef is fast disappearing from the family table. A farmer who kept a magnificent herd of Ruby Reds on the foothills of Exmoor watches his grandson buying Charolais-cross calves for £130 apiece, knowing full well that he will have to spend a small fortune to take them to 600kg. Grandfather raised his home-bred Devons mostly on grass.

I yearn for the days when I could go into almost any butcher's shop south of the A30 and buy South Devon beef with that pink pearly look, knowing that it had had little but mother's milk and grass. I do not intend to start a breed argument, simply to indulge in a little nostalgia. It is my belief that when this country returns to prosperity—and sanity—that genuine old British breeds like the South Devon and the Devon will regain their rightful place in the beef scene.

It is impossible to be exact when attempting to gauge public taste. According to the latest poll carried out by MORI on factors in choosing meat, taste and value for money, followed closely by price, were the most important considerations. Convenience—in contrast to my observations—influenced only half the people interviewed, while only 32 per cent were worried about their weight.

Nineteen per cent said they were eating less fat meat and 14 per cent thought they would be healthier if they did consume less fat. Twenty-five per cent were eating less sugar and 22 per cent less butter—bad news for Westcountry dairy farmers.

The upshot of all this, says Keith Roberts, chairman of the Meat and Livestock Commission, is that consumers are anxious about fat meat, just as they are about butter, salt and sugar. "The British meat and livestock industry has reacted positively to the pronounced trend in public preference for lean meat and in its own interests as well as those of the consumers, the industry will continue to move in that direction."

This would seem to spell a death-knell for all sire breeds except the Charolais and Limousin, a verdict which I refuse to accept. I do not accept minimum back fat as the ultimate criteria.

It seems to me that a few self-opinioniated nutritionists are helping to re-shape the entire meat industry (worth £75-million in steer beef alone to Devon and Cornwall livestock farmers).

I agree with Keith Roberts that lean meat should not be seen as a health hazard. On the other hand the whole country seems to be on the verge of going bananas over a bit of fat. Smokers go their own way to self destruction, regardless of public health warnings. Why not give the consuming public at least a choice of eating the meat of their choice. It cannot be all that harmful.

Jim Butcher

Built for aquatics

Dusk was closing in, but the surface of the road still mirrored the reeds beside me. Suddenly, only a few feet away, a water shrew surfaced and slid onto a water lily leaf. Its tiny body barely dented the leaf as it swung its head to and fro, nose twitching as it tested the air. Then, momentarily, the edge of the leaf curled and the water shrew dived, leaving the merest ripple to confirm that my eyes had not deceived me.

That was my first water shrew. Since then I have been fortunate in discovering a little more about their private lives.

For instance, they are extremely efficient underwater operators. When they dive, their close-knit fur entraps air bubbles, thus preventing their skin becoming wet and cold. It also gives built-in buoyancy. Whenever I watch one swimming below the surface I am always impressed by its silvery shimmer and beautiful streamlining. On the surface they bob about like mobile corks.

To give them more thrust through the water, their toes are fringed with small stiff hairs. The tail, flattened and tapered, is also fringed with hair, to act as a most efficient rudder.

Water shrews hunt aquatic insects, snails and even catch the occasional small fish. In dew-wet grass, these tiny mammals have many a wrestling match with large worms. I have seen a water shrew thrown completely off balance by a large and active earthworm.

These shrews spend most of the day and night in a frenzied search for food, with only an occasional rest back in the nest, to recharge the batteries. In woodland—for they are often found well away from water—they explore the damp recesses beneath fallen leaves for wood louse, beetles and many kinds of small, active invertebrates. Cress beds are a favourite habitat. Here the rich vegetation provides ample cover as they seek and catch water shrimps and insects among the tangled roots and stems. As with many man-made habitats though, change comes suddenly. Periodically the cress beds have to be cleared for replanting, and so the shrew population have to search for more durable, natural habitats.

Maybe that first one I saw was a refugee from a cleared cress bed, its tiny 15 gram body glistening with a season of good living.

Leslie Jackman

Life in a strike-bound community

It is all very well sitting in the peace and tranquillity of the Cornish countryside but how was it, I wondered, in the mining districts where most of the men, well over 100,000 of them, are out on strike.

How are the families coping? After nearly six months things must be getting desperate. There was only one way to find out and that was to go and see for myself.

When I told my friends I was going to stay with a mining family in the Durham district some of them were horrified, some even thought I was a traitor.

"I suppose you'll be standing in the picket lines yelling 'scab'," one said.

I had never visited a mining community before and had no idea what to expect. A journalist in Peterlee put me in touch with some mining families and within a day I had an invitation to stay with a family in the colliery village of Murton, some eight miles outside Durham.

In Murton, they told me, there were five pubs, five clubs and five churches and a population of 9,000 people whose lives depend almost entirely on the colliery which now stands silent, its great wheel dominating the village.

The Cornish links with mining areas all over the world are strong in Murton. A whole chunk of the village is called Cornwall after the Cornish miners who came to sink the shaft there in 1838–43.

The names of the streets and squares in that area are most familiar: Penzance, Bude, Trevone, Penryn and Tregony. There are still many people living there of Cornish descent and the older generation of women know how to bake a Cornish pasty.

The playing fields with tennis courts, the football ground, the bowling green and the huge Olympic-standard swimming pool in the village are all built by the miners for the miners "out of their pay notes" as they say. So, too, was the Miners' Hostel where the single miners retire in a very homely atmosphere.

Within minutes of arriving there I felt the unity and strength of the people who have long survived in work and play from the trust for and reliance on each other.

In the Miners' Welfare Hall, also built by the miners for the miners, 12 women who form the Murton Women's Support Group supply meals for the striking miners and their families.

Most days there are between three and five hundred gathered there to eat and meet. Food parcels are also put together for the single men who suffer most as they get no dole or social security and rely on those handouts and the generosity of their families to exist.

"Miners are used to giving—it is hard for us to take," one miner told me.

All the money for the food is raised from donations. Shops and individuals in Murton give generously. They all feel that if the pit closes down they too will go under. "We are solid in Murton," they boast all the time.

There is not time to stand and chat in the Welfare Hall and I was soon put to work washing up mountains of plates, chopping hundreds of tomatoes, trying to boil 200 eggs, buttering endless pieces of bread, and then serving out the food.

The 12 hard-working women under the leadership of Pam Blanchard, who is a magistrate and a gentle, efficient woman, are so different one to another in age, size and character and yet they work together in impressive efficiency and speed. There are no lady bountifuls doling out the charity, for everyone is in the same predicament and each is giving what he can to each. It's an intoxicating atmosphere of unity under stress.

I snatched pieces of conversation as we worked. "It's all very well when we gave up our holidays," one woman told me, "but when we have to deny the bairns their Christmas presents it will be hard. It's got to be over by then."

They were worried about buying clothes for the children to return to school. Concessions had been sought from schools who have compulsory uniform and funds set up to buy shoes. The children often go to their grandparents for their pocketmoney and their treats and get them from hard-earned pensions.

One of the greatest worries is the effect the violence on the picket lines will have on the youngsters and the children. Naturally, they all side with the pickets, since all their friends and relations are miners.

But their parents go to a great deal of trouble to combat a mistrust of law and order. One young father finding his five-year-old watching the television and being shocked by the police presence told him they were not really policemen but just people in fancy dress. Then he took the youngsters down to the local police station where he can talk to friendly policemen. "I don't want my children growing up to hate the police," he told me.

In Michael and Sylvia Rooney's house where I was staying I was welcomed with the warmth I had been told was very much part of Durham people. Though a perfect stranger, I was soon made to feel one of the family. There was no fuss, just common courtesy. Within hours I felt I had known them for years.

Sylvia retains the tradition of all miners' wives of working "like a Trojan". She not only keeps her house as neat as a pin, but enjoys working in her garden, which is a riot of colour, and goes out each day to feed and tidy for her crippled mother and help her single brother. She is often the careful minder for her beloved grandchild and the guardian and confidant of her two daughters.

Miners' wives are used to broken nights and irregular hours. They will never let a man leave the house for work without "putting up his bait" (making his sandwiches), and they like being there to welcome their husbands home with a hot dinner whether it be the middle of the night or the middle of the day. So they eat at differing times and are used to short nights and early rising.

Sylvia has always been the one in the family to manage the money matters, and she is now carefully eking out an existence on £15 for her and her husband and the one daughter who is still financially reliant on them.

They manage because they had savings, but these are beginning to run out now and they will soon have to start cutting back even more. So far they have still managed to eat quite well but their daughter cannot have new clothes and they cannot afford the bus rides to nearby Sunderland for shopping expeditions.

John Cummings, the leader of Easington District Council, in whose home I spent many happy hours, is a fifth generation miner of Murton. He works from dawn to dusk listening to people's problems, helping to sort them out.

He lives with his elderly parents who both avidly support the strike. His father was injured at the age of 14 in Murton pit; he nearly lost his leg. His mother, an ardent Roman Catholic, remembers the 1926 strike vividly.

One evening, in her soft voice, she read us an essay she has written about her childhood and the strike and half-way through she was stopped by her tears. We sat in respectful silence while she controlled herself and then read on.

It is not only the terrible way miners have suffered that she cries for, it is for her youth and the remembered closeness of the community. But she told me the unity has returned in the same way during the strike. She was not the only woman who told me: "We have not been so close for years as we are now."

George Cummings, well into his seventies, took me one afternoon to the allotments to see his racing pigeons which he has bred since he was a young man. He proudly showed me the cup he won for "topping the combine" (winning the highest prize in the area). He calls his pigeons "canny birds". In Durham district canny always means grand—the very best.

It was the next day as I sat in the Underground train in London that to my horror I felt tears rolling down my face. A great sadness had swept over me for the divisions in society, for the hatred and the violence, the lack of understanding, the cruelty of man to man, the manipulation and loss of communication and increase of force and dwindling of gentle persuasion.

Sarah Foot

WINTER

Steaming down to Kingswear

As a boy, grazing knees and scuffing shoes scrambing along embankments, my dream was to be a train driver. I recently had the good fortune to spend a day with the footplate crew of Lydham Manor on the Torbay and Dartmouth Railway.

The locomotive shone resplendent in Brunswich green, its elegant line set off with the attractive copper and brass embellishments that so typified the engines of the Great Western.

General manager Barry Cogar introduced me to driver Roger Gingell and fireman Carl Pittam and we all climbed into the cab.

The locomotive eased gently back onto its train of chocolate and cream coaches which formed the 10.30 a.m. to Kingswear.

The level crossing barriers south of Paignton station lowered to stop road traffic; the starter signal dropped with a clatter giving us right of way; leaving our locomotive panting at the leash.

Roger Gingell puts the reverser into forward gear and "blows" the brake off. Lydham Manor gives a sharp, spine-tingling whistle as the regulator is eased open and she pulls away in easy strides.

Carl Pittam shovels more coal into the hungry fire box. By the end of the day he can shift anything from one ton up to two tons during peak season. Driver Gingell gets the all clear from the guard and opens the regulator to do battle with the stiff two-and-a-half mile climb to Churston.

On a summer's day, the crew tells you, the communal waft of sun-tan oil hits the nose like a fist as the train curves above the red sands strewn with bronzing beauties. They rarely glimpse a topless bather—the approach of a panting steam engine seems sufficiently intimidating to cause a coy, quick, panic-stricken cover up.

Now, with winter approaching, the water looks less inviting. Torbay is a grey expanse of beaten pewter. A sure sign that the season is over is the steady removal of beach huts, the deserted acres of camp and caravan sites, and the brooding storm clouds mustering over this palm-treed holiday playground.

The exhaust beat of the engine deepens as it struggles with the gradient. It is a rich, throaty bark whose tone changes with the contours. In cuttings it snaps back sharp and staccato while on open ground it is a rounded, rich sound—repetitive, reassuring and music to the ear.

The wheels of the 4-6-0 slip slightly on rails salted by the damp sea air the night before. People in bungalow kitchens wave as our re-incarnation of God's Wonderful Railway chuffs placidly past the bottom of their gardens.

It's good to have friends. Particularly during what has been one of the railway's most difficult summers. The drought triggered off a few lineside fires and the coal strike caused engines to burn inferior fuel which in turn resulted in an embarrassing fall-out of clinker and smoke dust. Normally the locos consume nothing but the best South Wales steam coal—but this season they have considered themselves lucky to have obtained stocks of household coal from Nottinghamshire.

"We are selling nostalgia," said Barry Cogar, as Lydham Manor breasted the summit and steamed into Churston station with its seven-coach train.

"This is really an entertainment business. We are providing a service but it's not for the railway enthusiast as such, it's for people on holiday and locals who find the line a useful way to travel between Paignton and Kingswear."

Arguably one of the most picturesque preserved railways in the country, it offers the contrasting scenery of Torbay and the River Dart coupled with the novelty of a steam train.

I lean out of the cab as we drift down towards the mossy darkness of Greenway Tunnel, elbow resting nonchalantly on the ledge, grease-top cap pulled tightly about the ears for fear of it flying into the bracken-covered embankment.

Suddenly the single-bore gloom of the tunnel swallows us up. Billows of pink-blushed smoke squeeze between the brick-arched roof and the cab.

The cab glows orange as it reflects the anger of the fire, and our faces resemble the cast of Dante's inferno—red, flickering, almost demonic.

The cacophony inside the tunnel is suddenly subdued as we burst into daylight and glide over Maypole Viaduct.

The first views of the languid River Dart emerge through the trees on our right. Surrounding hills are eclipsed by mist as rain blows in from the west.

Being the first of the day, at Britannia Halt driver Gingell stops his train to allow the gatekeeper to get off. During the winter the old-style GWR crossing gates will be removed and modern lifting barriers installed. People queueing for the ferry cannot resist jumping from their cars to snatch a few instamatic photographs as we steam serenely by.

Time for a quick coffee and piece of cake in the station buffet guarded by a life-size cardboard cut-out of frock-coated Brunel. Then back up in the cab for the return journey.

The irony of life on the footplate is that the body is always assaulted by extremes of temperature—the top half frozen while the bottom half bakes. In our case, travelling tender first, our backs were roasted by the open fire box while our fronts absorbed a good soaking from the sou'westerly.

"When people talk of the romance of railways," shouted Barry Cogar over the sound of steam and lash of the rain, "they don't realise some of the difficult conditions the men have to work under."

Roger Malone

Winter moths

With most of November gone, and with a high proportion of the leaves from the trees, it was easy to imagine that Nature was going to sleep. But five minutes in the garden quickly dispelled that idea.

Brushing a few of the leaves from a border, I exposed the red-purple buds of hellebore pushing through the ground, ready to provide us with our Christmas roses. Digging up a seedling nettle, I accidentally uprooted a daffodil, exposing new vigorous roots over six inches long. In my office tonight I had more evidence that Nature never sleeps.

The gales and rains of the day had temporarily eased when my attention was drawn to a faint fluttering at my lighted window.

A frail moth with medium brown upper, and paler lower, wings was obviously fascinated by the beam from my desk light.

It was a November moth, an inconspicuous creature that chooses to reach the finale of its life when nights are long and often unpleasant. Its eggs are yellow when laid, but then turn dark crimson. Surprisingly, they blend sufficiently with the bark of the various trees on which they are laid for enough to survive and produce caterpillars in the spring.

After a time, an even smaller moth arrived at the window, grey-brown in colour with dark lines crossing its wings. This was a winter moth and very definitely a male. The female of this species is virtually wingless, remaining close by where it hatched from its chrysalis until it is visited by a male, after which it lays its eggs on trees and bushes.

Its survival depends entirely on the effectiveness of its colour camouflage blending with the bark on which it rests.

Bob Holmes

The Mad Axeman's escape

Eighteen years ago this month the Westcountry was buzzing with the news that Frank Mitchell—the Mad Axeman—was on the loose from Dartmoor Prison.

Mitchell's flight, followed around a fortnight later on Boxing Day by a further five prisoners, brought Lord Mountbatten to Dartmoor in the course of a valuable inquiry he was undertaking on behalf of the Home Office. There are far fewer escapes from the Moor these days than in the past, thanks to a much greater tightening of security arrangements after the Mountbatten inquiry.

Mitchell's escape was as unexpected, though, as it was embarrassing. For only a fortnight earlier, a deeply concerned resident living at Baggator, near Peter Tavy, had phoned the Press asking if it was true that a man whom one of her friends had identified as "The Mad Axeman" was, indeed, employed with an outside prisoner working party so far from the gaol itself. "Yes," confirmed the prison, but Mitchell was now "as gentle as a kitten".

Mitchell was being treated with more than usual generosity by the prison staff: he had managed to convince many that he was in no way insane, and that his behaviour had been outrageous to draw public attention to his personal plight. He'd certainly succeeded. What the prison authorities did not know, however, was that Frank Mitchell was also planning his freedom long before the due date. By methods which have only been broadly hinted at, Mitchell had persuaded a fellow prisoner to use his influence on his friends to "spring" him from gaol.

Mitchell, by pre-arrangement, simply walked away from the Baggator working party one cold, wet December afternoon, and was never seen again. He apparently told the officer in charge that he was going to feed the ponies. The following day his prison clothing was found in a layby at Crockernwell, miles from the prison, together with a large knife.

Police, Royal Marine Commandos and even a Scots regiment, then stationed at Plymouth, took part in the search for the man but to no avail. I recall visiting the Baggator area with a London Times reporter some days after the event and listening, in quiet amazement, to the sound of the bagpipes played by a lone piper above Baggator, while down below, the kilted regiment searched through bog and scrubland for traces of Frank Mitchell.

But tales of the Mad Axeman's activities in and around the Tavistock area began to emerge with such rapidity, that soon a legend was built up. Mitchell, a man of considerable strength, was said to have lifted, single-handed, the rear end of a police car: he kept budgerigars in his prison cell, was said to have ridden the wild ponies on the Moor: there were reports that he was a regular at a local hostelry, and that he had a girl-friend in the village. I recall with other reporters following up a story that he had an account at a local betting shop—our inquiries came to nothing.

Some of the stories were later denied. But the fact remained, Mitchell had done what very few had ever, before or since; he had not only escaped from Dartmoor Prison, but he had appeared to vanish from the face of the earth.

Just twelve months after the escape, I was sent to London to find Mitchell's parents, and interview them—if I could. Apart from the fact that Mitchell came from the East End of the city, I had little information to direct me.

Fortune, however, favoured me on that bright December morning in 1967, for at the very first East End police station where I made my inquiries, a Devon-born sergeant was in charge. He called a taxi for me, spoke quietly and seriously to the driver, and set me on my way.

When the car pulled up outside the Mitchells' home, the taxi driver told me that he would wait for 15 minutes only, and would then come in to check on what was happening. It sounded all too dramatic for me, but I had no choice except to agree. The Mitchells proved to be a delightful couple, with a daughter who was as worried as her parents about her brother's whereabouts. And, sure enough, after 15 minutes, the taxi driver came in, waggled a finger in my direction, and brought the brief interview to an end—there and then. Everyone seemed to understand, except myself, the unwritten laws, the freemasonry of the East End.

They believed Mitchell was still alive and well—but later stories seemed to suggest that he had been removed, a nuisance to his friends who had become his captors. One day, perhaps, we may know the truth behind his disappearance, but, summer or winter, I can never visit the Baggator area on Dartmoor without recalling the skirl of pipes and the tale of the one that got away.

James Mildren

Miss Fookes camps out with the Marines

"However many men did you sleep with then?" a colleague enquired of me recently.

"Quite a lot" was my rejoinder—and in case anyone thinks that this heralds what would be described as 'steamy confessions' in less refined newspapers than this one, let me hurriedly explain. The second night of the visit to 3 Commando Brigade RM involved sleeping out in the field in a ten-man tent. Among my companions were Lt.-Col. Rupert van der Horst, the CO of 42 Commando, Rear Admiral Higgins, formerly Commodore of HMS Drake, Earl Attlee and Roger Gale, MP.

Earlier in the evening we had all stumbled along a snowy track beneath the hard glitter of brilliant stars to see a night demonstration—an eerie experience as night skiers suddenly emerged and tiny sounds carried startlingly long distances in the cold calm atmosphere

—a reminder of the hazard of giving away one's position when fighting in sub-zero temperatures.

Throughout the trip we were all glad of the excellent Arctic kit provided for us, and not surprised to learn that it is a constant topic of conversation—especially when someone finds what they think is a better item than that officially provided. There is, in fact, constant evaluation of kit and equipment in conditions where hypothermia is not the preserve of the aged, or the poor, but an ever-present danger to be guarded against at all times. One of the most extraordinary hazards is that men can over-heat when carrying heavy packs and ski-ing, sweat profusely and find it turning to ice when they cool down.

At Hindseter men from "L" Company, 42 Commando, demonstrated how a team skis across country with a pathfinder in the front, and each man having a task to perform strung out behind and a man at the back towing a sledge or "pulk" with heavier equipment. At the beginning of each winter deployment, every marine has basic training in skiing and survival techniques before they move on to training in military skills which culminate in a full-scale NATO exercise.

The Commandos are ably supported by various other units which comprise the Brigade, and we were fortunate, by dint of a fair amount of travelling by civilian coach, to see something of their activities. Thus on the third day of our visit we moved north-westwards to Setnesmoen where 29 Commando Regiment Royal Artillery are situated. We arrived in swirling snow to receive a warm welcome and briefing from the CO, Lt.-Col. Ian Durie, before we ventured outside to see a demonstration involving the deployment of Rapier missiles, Blowpipe missiles and the so-called 105mm light gun.

There was an opportunity to ride snow scooters which would have rejoiced the heart of any schoolchild, and rejoiced mine as well. I rode pillion, and then took the controls under the kindly eye of Sergeant Porter from Plymouth, who risked his neck riding behind while I careered about—at one point striking out into deep snow, and being temporarily blinded by spray on my goggles.

At Dombas, the headquarters of 59 Independent Commando Squadron, Royal Engineers, enthusiastically commanded by Major Tim Hoddinott, the demonstrations we saw brought out the varied

Sarah Foot helps with the washing up at Murton Miners' welfare hall.
Photo: Ian Dobson

Lost sheep near Dotton.
Photo: James Ravilious

4930 "Hagley Hall" and 7819 "Hinton Manor" climbing Dainton bank between Totnes and Newton Abbot with the "Great Western Limited".
Photo: Mark S. Wilkins

H.M.S. Torquay, the frigate built in 1956, paying her farewell visit to Torbay on being retired from the active fleet.
Photo: Torbay News Agency

role of the Engineers in supporting the Brigade. One such involved us scrambling down a very steep river bank, where we watched a young diver disappear down a forbidding rectangle cut out of the ice. He re-emerged triumphantly bearing a large salmon destined to be eaten later that night. The serious purpose was to show us what is involved in trying to destroy underwater structures in a war situation and in such bleak conditions.

We also saw an exercise in bridge demolition (in theory, I should add) and I was told later that one of the men who demonstrated the role of mines in the operation, Cpl. Walker, had actually lost a leg when a mine blew up in the Falklands. You just would not know and he walks, runs and dances with his artificial limb—he was not above discarding it suddenly as a mischievous trick.

When we reached our final day we found ourselves back at Gardemoen where we had begun. Our tour there included a visit to 3 Commando Brigade's Air Squadron. Not for the first time I was brought up against the hellish difficulties of operating helicopters in very cold conditions. We saw a helicopter undergoing maintenance and were shown some vital rubber parts perished in the cold, and told how easy it is for oil to freeze solid and ground a helicopter completely.

Last, but definitely not least, we glimpsed the myriad activities of the Commando Logistic Regiment which provides kit, equipment, food supplies, transport and fuel for the Brigade. Nothing and no-one would function without them. Most fascinating to me was a stretcher for use in remote areas utilising a man's own skis and ski-poles. We also went inside a field dressing station complete with its own de-contamination unit.

I recognise that we saw but a fraction of what is involved in the Commandos' deployment in Norway but it was enough to impress upon us the sheer professionalism of the Royal Marines and the serious way in which they tackle their vital task of defending the Northern Flank from possible Soviet attack. It is a vital role probably not readily appreciated by the public at large.

Janet Fookes, MP
for Plymouth Drake

Zennor as a Christmas present

When my husband asked me what I would like for Christmas, I told him I wanted to spend a day at Zennor. Not only was my wish granted, but it came to fruition earlier than I anticipated.

Why is it that the brutal coastline around Land's End has become a shrine for me? I only ever go in the winter. There is hardly anyone there. The holiday houses are identifiable by their drawn curtains, the perfection of decoration and their empty lost look. Now the area is given back to those who work the land and provide the services.

The Zennor countryside has a way of ripping away pretence, making one face up to true values, reviving only those things that really matter. There, where the granite-strewn moors meet the checker-board fields hedged with boulders, uncovered and untreed, that lead onto the aquamarine sea, cold and bitter and shining bright, one's very being seems to be threatened and then revitalised.

We were lucky that the weather was so perfect. I love Zennor in rain, hail storms, thunder and lightning but this was a day of bright clear winter sunshine. The wind was there (is it ever not?) but the sunlight pierced the mist and made the outlines of mines, boulders and cliffs all the more sharp and harrowing.

We drove from St. Ives to Zennor, along that twisting road which I have long claimed offers the most outstanding views in Cornwall. Every house and every hedge seems to be made from the largest chunks of granite a man could possibly move.

Above the road the moor glowers down to those small fields and the sea beyond. Coming upon Zennor, each time, is a special kind of surprise. In the church you can sit and listen to the wind whistling in the tower above and through the cracks in door and ceiling and imagine it is the "cold and insatiate crying from the tangled bay" of the Mermaid of Zennor whose image is carved on one of the only remaining 15th century bench ends.

She was, according to legend, a beautiful woman who sat in the back of the church listening to one of the choristers, Matthew Trewhella. One evening she lured him into the sea at a spot now named Mermaid's Cove. She was a very famous mermaid, the only one mentioned by name in the Encyclopedia Britannica.

Not far from the village of Zennor we drove through the hamlet of Botallack where the sound in the wind is not so reminiscent of the song of mermaids but more of the crunch of the tin miners' boots as they walked through the village down to the mining buildings known as the Crowns where the work went on hundreds of fathoms under the sea.

These buildings are now being restored as a memorial to the work carried out in the area.

So my present went on being unwrapped as we moved from familiar and long-loved parts of Cornwall to some I have never been to before. For the first time we drove down to Cape Cornwall. Here men worked on the roads, repairing the damage of the holiday visitors and the elements. Apart from the workmen there was no one else about.

Back through the narrow lanes we went to St. Just. Looking up at the church tower we saw four seagulls perched on each pinnacle of the tower, as if they too were carved of granite.

I have to go to Land's End whenever I am in the area and this was no exception.

If you stand looking out from the cliff face, you can easily forget the commercial exercise that must take place at such a popular tourist trap.

The light that shafted down across that open seascape between Land's End and the Isles of Scilly was dramatic and yet dream-like. In the sound of the wind that bit into our faces I could hear the bells of the submerged churches that once existed in the land of Lyonesse. If I ever go to that cliff face and can no longer believe in the legends that abound there then I will know that I am truly lost.

On the lanes between Land's End and Porthcurno the leafless trees were wreathed in garlands of Old Man's Beard, more beautiful than any Christmas tree decoration.

My present revealed new aspects as we wended our way down the valley following the stream that leads to Lamorna Cove, another of Cornwall's more hidden beauty places.

From Lamorna we drove on to Mousehole where I expected to be sad, remembering the terrible loss of life in the lifeboat accident of Christmas time 1981. But to my surprise there was a large decorated dragon in the harbour and people were obviously going about the business of preparing for Christmas celebration. Another example of Cornishmen and women recovering from tragic circumstances with a sort of defiance.

In Newlyn the harbour was busy, workmanlike and not at all tourist-spoiled. Boats were coming and going in the last light of afternoon, Christmas lights in the shape of two great bells were being tested on the pier.

The last wrapper of my present exposed that great sight of St. Michael's Mount as we drove along the waterfront of Penzance. The sun had gone, the greyness of evening had fallen, this was the last offering in my multi-faceted Christmas present, the turreted outline of Cornwall's greatest shrine.

Sarah Foot

Does Mrs. Thatcher have any regrets?

Ten years on, life at the top is not all that was intended.

Mostly, yes. But not quite. When Margaret Thatcher became Tory leader in 1975, she was consumed by many determinations, not least a resolve to avoid a confrontation with the miners at almost any price.

She was still firmly of this mind when she arrived at 10, Downing Street, four years later.

While Joe Gormley was at the head of the NUM, the path to industrial peace was not all that hard to tread. Few union leaders have achieved more for their rank-and-file than he did. He knew how far to push, but he also knew when it was politic to call it a day. So these two disparate characters got along remarkably well.

Then along came Arthur Scargill, a fanatic with a deadly purpose to use his industrial muscle to bring down her Government. For such a cool, confident person, the Prime Minister over-reacted and appointed Ian McGregor, hot from the diminishing steel furnaces, to head the National Coal Board. From then on, the confrontation that Maggie had so genuinely wanted to avoid, was inevitable. I sometimes wonder whether she now half regrets her impetuosity.

There was one stern lesson, though, that Mrs. Thatcher learned from the last days of the hapless Heath regime. No Government can afford to take on a major union—and lose. Hence the present war of attrition, not against the mining industry, which has much to thank the present Government for, but against Arthur Scargill and his militant minions.

And what of the other irritant, Ken Livingstone? Even some of her own Party supporters believe that again the Prime Minister over-reacted. Abolishing the GLC and the Metropolitan Councils is seeming more and more like using a sledge hammer to quash a passing nuisance. It may have sounded like a good idea at the time of the General Election, but now, nearly two years on, Ministers have still not come up with all the detailed answers on what to put in their place.

For some reason or other, Conservative Governments are attracted to local government reform like moths to a flame, and their commitment to take more power away from Whitehall produces at times very strange manifestations.

Patrick Jenkin, the Environment Secretary and one of the nicest politicians in the business, is no match for the likes of Ken Livingstone in this latest campaign, and it is not without note that Conservative Central Office has virtually given up the uneven struggle of presenting a viable case.

Ten years on, it is not hard to find other contradictions between Tory philosophy and Tory practice.

Slashing inflation, Mrs. Thatcher can chalk up as one of her great achievements, and nobody should try to decry the inestimable benefits this has brought to individuals and to industry. But what possesses Ministers to indulge in inflationary moves like forcing up water rates, more than double the need in some areas? I applaud the five Westcountry Conservative MPs who refused to support the Government on this ten days ago, but what of the others, who plodded meekly through the lobbies? (I excuse Alan Clark, who was probably in Bongo Bongo land).

That's what comes of precedents.

With remarkably little opposition within its own ranks, the Government got away with a tax on gas, well above the needs of inflation, that did considerable damage not only to household budgets, but to a vast number of firms.

I remember taxing Mrs. Thatcher about this at the time, and, from one who is normally engagingly frank, her answer erred very much on the glib and the bland.

Gas, electricity prices, water rates. What next, one wonders, in the drive against inflation?

Of course, she did not sanction the prosecution of Clive Ponting in the Belgrano case. Even the inexperienced Neil Kinnock should know that this is the prerogative of the Attorney General, acting not in his Ministerial but in his legal capacity, and no one else.

But two very simple facts emerge from the complex issues revolving round the sinking of the Belgrano and the Court case.

Clive Ponting abused his trust, and has undermined the vital and historic relationship between Ministers and the Civil Service.

For its part, the Government has held back on some of the facts about the sinking of the Belgrano, and, wittingly or otherwise, has misled Parliament on more than one occasion.

There is nothing new about the latter, of course. Several years ago, a Cabinet Minister, who remains a leading figure in the Commons, denied point blank at the Dispatch Box a story I had filed about Devonport Dockyard.

Two days later, a White Paper, which must have been at the printers a week before, confirmed every word that I had written.

Ah! well, That's politics.

L. K. Way,
Our Lobby Correspondent 1947–81

Challenge from a reader

I'm afraid the article by your ex Lobby correspondent, L. K. Way, is seriously flawed in some of its assumptions.

Mrs. Thatcher did not come to power in 1979 "with a resolve to avoid a confrontation with the miners at almost any price". On the contrary, she was armed with a report prepared by Nicholas Ridley (now the Transport Minister) which outlined precisely the plans to be made in preparation for taking on the miners again. These included building up large stocks of coal, making preparations for easy conversion of power stations to oil firing, organising large fleets of road hauliers to carry the coal that would be "blacked" by the railway workers and to start the dispute at the end of the winter. As we all know, this plan has been followed precisely.

She did not "over-react" in appointing Ian McGregor. Having first confirmed that he had no compunction about butchering industry by putting him in charge of British Steel, she then appointed him to the Coal Board to initiate a confrontation with the miners. She had two previous opportunities to confront the miners, in 1982 and 1983, but she drew back as she was not yet fully prepared. Mr. Scargill warned the miners that the time would shortly come that they would have to stand and fight to save their industry and he was exactly right.

Mr. Way also described Mr. Scargill as a "fanatic with a deadly purpose". May I remind him that Mr. Scargill was leader of the Yorkshire miners for ten years when there was absolutely no trouble in the Yorkshire area, apart from the national strike. Some fanatic! No, the fanatic with a deadly purpose was clearly Mrs. Thatcher. As she has shown, and the Chancellor has said, they will pay any price to defeat the miners. That price is catastrophe for the balance of payments and more than decimation of the value of the pound.

As for Conservative governments being "attracted to local government reform like moths to a candle," the most positive reform faithfully promised in their election manifesto was of local rates—just the first promise to be contemptuously discarded when the election was won.

Mr. Way wants to know why gas, electricity prices and water rates have been forced up artificially, despite the effect on inflation. The answer is clear. The Chancellor has been unable to get Government spending under control as they promised, so they have raised these prices to reduce the public sector borrowing requirement to make money available for tax cuts for the wealthy.

In conclusion, it would be interesting to know why L. K. Way fails to name the ex-Cabinet Minister who lied at the Dispatch Box when he denied a story filed by Mr. Way? It couldn't possibly be because he is motivated by a party political affiliation.

David Gorbutt
Chairman Devon Labour Party
Old Station House, Brentor

Inviting crime

I am glad to see that all hell is still being raised all over Devon and Cornwall at the multitude of sub-post office closures that are threatened.

One must not blame the Post Office, but their governmental masters who have given them a brief so insensitive to public needs.

But for a Head Postmaster to suggest to protestors that people could act as agents to collect the pensions of elderly people must be dangerous, as one action group has pointed out.

We live in an age when banks and shops use security firms which are in effect private police forces, so organised and violent have robbers become, and when no old lady carrying a handbag with a few shillings in it is safe on our pavements.

Neighbours collecting pensions for a group of elderly people will quickly become targets for criminals.

John Theobald

Christmas Eve in the cathedrals

Tonight (Christmas Eve)—this most special of nights—the two great cathedrals of Devon and Cornwall will, for a while, be plunged into darkness, and in the two buildings, about 3,000 people will wait with seasonal anticipation.

In Truro, beneath those three towering lance-like spires, suddenly will come, as crystal clear as a frosty night, the voice of a chorister singing the first verse of "Once in Royal David's City".

The choir, carrying lanterns with candles in them, red-robed and surpliced white, will join in the second verse, and then the congregation, and the festival of nine lessons and carols for use upon Christmas Eve will have begun.

Some 90 miles away, an hour earlier, the far more ancient Exeter Cathedral, packed so tight that not one more could possibly squeeze in—not with today's safety regulations anyway—will also have been in darkness.

There, two lads, white albs over their scarlet cassocks, each carrying lighted candles, will emerge from behind the high altar, and sing the announcement of the birth of Christ.

"Today" they sing, "for us, the King of Heaven hath deigned to be born of a virgin."

And the choir responds: "That He might restore lost mankind. The Angelic Host rejoiceth for that eternal salvation hath appeared to the children of men."

The lights will go on, flooding the Nave and the aisles, illuminating the whiteness of the Purbeck marble, and the great Grandisson service will be underway.

Both these services will be continuing traditions that have their roots in the misty pasts of centuries ago.

Whether or not the festival of nine lessons and carols was actually "invented" in Cornwall is probably impossible to say.

What is known for sure is that it was, "after ancient tradition" revived at Truro Cathedral by the then Bishop—later to become Archbishop—Edward White Benson in 1880.

Only then, of course, Truro Cathedral as we know it now, did not exist.

In fact, in 1880, the cathedral was nothing more than a humble wooden building, one that was to serve as both parish church and cathedral for seven years.

It was put up on October 11 of that year because of the demolition of most of St. Mary's Church on which site the cathedral was to be built.

The Bishopric of Truro had been founded some four years earlier, and Edward Benson, Residentiary Canon and Chancellor of Lincoln Cathedral, had been enthroned as the first Bishop of Truro in 1877.

By 1880, when he revived the form of service for Christmas Eve that was in later years to spread throughout the world, the foundation stone of the new cathedral had been laid, but the job of creating a beautiful Gothic building had only just started.

Between 700 and 1,000 people will fill Truro Cathedral tonight to listen to the lessons, hear the carols—some of them specifically Cornish—and sing the Christmas hymns.

The Dean said that there were probably earlier forms along similar lines to the present service, but Archbishop Benson, over a century ago, had brought them together to form the present one.

And it is nice to think that that service not only became part of the cathedral's tradition, but a good Cornish export in the bargain.

Of course, the origins of the Grandisson service in Exeter Cathedral are much older, but strangely perhaps not in the form it presently takes and which attracts a congregation of 2,000 with people waiting patiently outside in case some with tickets do not turn up.

What Bishop Grandisson did as long ago as 1337 was to issue an "ordinale" that was included in the service that took place at, or near, midnight on Christmas Eve.

It is that act of the two choirboys making the announcement of the birth of Christ which Bishop Grandisson introduced into a service, which in those days would have been Mattins and which would have been followed by Mass.

Explained Canon John Thurmer, Chancellor of Exeter Cathedral: "It was a little dramatic ceremony to mark the beginning of the Christmas festival. It might be that Bishop Grandisson experienced this somewhere else, possibly on the Continent."

The little ceremony has not gone on being observed every Christmas Eve over the centuries.

Canon Thurmer said that it would have continued until the Reformation, and then ceased.

But a form of it was revived in the early part of this century—round about 1930.

Then it was inserted into evensong, and it was not until about 15 years ago that the Grandisson service, as it is known and so much enjoyed in today's form, was started.

The music for the service was composed by Sir Thomas Armstrong, one of the cathedral's distinguished organists.

The service now is certainly a crowd-puller with its mixture of music, readings, procession and ceremony, such as the blessing of the crib and the lighting of the Christmas tree.

"If we put it on twice we could probably fill the Cathedral twice over," said Canon Thurmer.

What both occasions have—and I know them well, having sung as a lad in the Truro Cathedral choir, and having attended the Grandisson service a number of times—is the ability not only to evoke the atmosphere of Christmas, but, as acts of worship, to symbolise the real essence and significance of the Christian festival.

Derek Lean

Great full-backs from Penryn

At a time when Cornish rugby is going through one of the leanest of periods, the followers of the game in Cornwall will find pleasure in the selection of Chris Martin as the England full-back to play against Ireland on January 19.

But what is also of interest is that, as a former and very young *Penryn* player, he follows a tradition of football that can hardly be matched in any other place of similar size anywhere in the land.

He is, for example, the *second* English full-back to come from this tiny place (two decades ago, Roger Hosen played for England): and when a year or so back I was writing a book to mark the centenary of rugby in Cornwall one of the things that struck me was how rich Penryn had especially been in full-backs.

Graham Bate was another (in 1967–68 when Penryn won all their games and scored 534 points, Bate got 318 of them), and the current Penryn full-back Paul Winnan, is a player who for Cornwall, St. Ives and Penryn has brought me as much pleasure in his play as any Cornish player I have seen over the past few years.

Not that Penryn has had a monopoly of Cornish international full-backs.

The finest of them was unquestionably John Jackett, of Falmouth (13 caps), a player of quite daunting commitment.

It is said of him that when young he used to go to the Falmouth ground alone, place buckets around the touchline and touch-kick directly into them (who now in rugby has such an interest?)

And another, within my own pleasurable memory, is John Collins of Camborne.

From the touchline, he looked frail; but on the field he had the courage of five; and when he kicked for touch you could hear the thump two parishes away! And if I live to be 100, I doubt I'll ever have a rugby memory to equal the one that came to me, week after week, a few years back, of John Collins's carefully setting-out the corner flags for a Camborne club game.

It epitomised for me, as nothing else has ever done the love the Cornish entertain for rugby football . . .

But to come back to young Chris Martin and Penryn (for I have digressed), the other thing about Penryn and rugby is that its burghers have made three *rugby players* Freemen of the Borough

(Hosen, Vic Roberts—the best player of the bunch—Ken Plummer) and it is a nice and proper genuflection and appreciation of what the game of rugby has meant to my native county and to Penryn.

Things may not seem well now in Cornish football, but there's a glorious tradition to seek to emulate: and the choice, at long last, of another Cornish international could, possibly, be the catalyst.

I so hope so . . . .

Tom Salmon
A letter to the editor

The Okehampton By-pass I
Keep the National Park inviolate

England is a small country. Both sides argue the case, alternatively that we cannot spare farmland and that our remaining unspoilt heritage of natural beauty has to be carefully preserved.

I believe that Dartmoor is more precious than farmland because there is much less of it. Dartmoor is often called England's Last Wilderness. It is special. Moreover, the periphery of the Moor, where the rivers come tumbling down in deep, wooded valleys, is among the very best. The argument that the Okehampton by-pass would cause little damage as it would "only just" be built within the park is particularly misleading.

Almost all of Okehampton Park, which would be sliced through by the by-pass, partly on viaducts, is included in the National Park.

I am not an extreme preservationist. I have accused Lady Sayer of sometimes being too militant and in danger of turning moderate opinion away from a commonsense cause. But on this topic I find myself at one with her. The National Park would be the "monstrous choice," and if it were adopted one would have to wonder why we bother to have a National Park system at all.

Remember that the National Park route has already been officially chosen, and it is only because of one factor that the debate continues: Bluebell Wood and East Hill are officially-recognised "open spaces", and the compulsory purchase order for the by-pass route across them is subject to Parliamentary procedure. It is now in the hands of Members of both Houses. And lest the argument is that a choice once made should be respected, those trying to defend the National Park will remind you most strongly that Meldon Reservoir was virtually built by trick.

The planning assessor, who was appointed to assist the engineering inspector, said: "In my judgment the planning arguments against the proposal are very substantial. The rarest beauty of the Moor belongs to its fringes, not to the upland wastes; and the steep-sided valley by which the West Okement leaves it is one of the loveliest. It is all the more valuable because so much of this part of Dartmoor is now occupied (and in no little degree marred) by military use."

When you visit the reservoir, your first reaction might well be that it is itself a thing of beauty. Steeply landlocked sheets of water always have their attraction. But when you look down at the continuing valley dwarfed below, you realise what a treasure has indeed been thrown away. There is nothing else like it.

Move sufficiently downstream to enjoy the full natural beauty of this rugged stream cutting its way through the steeply-wooded landscape, and then you are just where the proposed A30 is planned to dominate. The scale of the landscape is at once so grandiose and so delicate as to make it impossible to build anything large there without destroying it.

The by-pass would not be confined to a narrow band of land gently cut into the hillside as was the Southern Railway, whose passengers were deprived of the best views to prevent greater damage being done to the landscape. Even the railway's Meldon Viaduct, with its slender lattice girders allowing you to see straight through it, had amazingly little impact, indeed looking almost a part of Dartmoor.

On its way from the present A30 to Fatherford, just over a mile to the east of Okehampton, to Hughslade, about 2½ miles to the west, the proposed by-pass would commit outrage upon outrage, running almost the entire distance within the National Park.

Of course Okehampton is frequently spoilt by the pressure of traffic in its midst, but I doubt whether that does more damage to the town than would the A30 effectively creating a barrier between it and the Moor.

Cornwall, of course, urgently needs a better A30. But wrongs do not aggregate into rights. This part of Dartmoor has been given terrible treatment, and later generations are bound to judge us harshly if we cap it with the destruction of the gem that remains.

What of the alternate route? Part of it cuts through good scenery, too, though nothing as unique as what lies in the National Park. Much of the farmland to the north is low grade, and it is hard to believe that its loss would be a national catastrophe.

David St John Thomas

The Okehampton By-pass II
A vital need that must go south

Surely it is unnecessary to present a case for an Okehampton by-pass—the last town to be relieved of traffic—between the national network starting at Whiddon Down, seven miles from the town, and Land's End.

Situated on the main spine road to the South-West, Okehampton suffers an ever increasing pounding by heavy vehicles and holiday traffic. No longer can it be said that the by-pass is only required for a few week-ends at the height of the holiday season. The whole peninsula depends on road transport—passenger, goods and private—and the failure to improve communications has a serious and damaging effect on development and jobs in West Devon and the whole of Cornwall.

The possibility of a container port at Falmouth, and any industrial growth, can only add to the already unacceptable situation in our town and adds weight to the urgency for a final decision and the construction of a new road.

Noises were being made even before the second World War that the only solution to the growing traffic problem would be a by-pass. After the war the growth in traffic made the need for a by-pass even more urgent. Slowly the effect of this increase in the number of vehicles, mainly at week-ends, was having an impact on Saturday trading. The number of stalls in Fore Street diminished, until there was only one; the cattle market suffered from the difficulty of getting into and out of Okehampton and this was a major factor in its demise; even shopping patterns changed, and Saturday afternoons are now very quiet times for traders.

In the early 60s, the railway started closing lines and road transport became the only means of moving freight. The need for a by-pass was constantly stressed, but the problems of where it should go were good reasons for leaving it until later, and so we saw by-passes built for Honiton and Cullompton, Bodmin and Launceston; and Okehampton gained a reputation for its traffic problems, and a place to be avoided.

The A30 came tantalisingly close—seven miles away—and the route was agreed to Tongue End Cross, just two miles from the town. But that stretch was included in the Okehampton by-pass inquiry. A decision has been made on this stretch much to the relief of terrified villagers at Sticklepath, and the delay resulted in many serious accidents, including fatalities.

The traffic through Okehampton has now reached frightening levels. No longer is it week-end chaos: heavy trucks rumble through the town all day and every day, causing damage to property and destroying a quality of life we are entitled to expect living in a very small town in rural Devon. Sadly, there are no inner relief roads nor any possibility of diverting traffic. The trunk road remains a solid division between the north and south of the town.

The 1975 consultation resulted in a clear majority in favour of the southern route. Note the year: 1975. The public inquiry was held in 1979, and it was a very thorough inquiry, not Department of Transport "window dressing" as has been suggested. Mr. Fay carried out this inquiry with dignity, often under considerable strain, needing to attempt to retain control of his inquiry.

Of course "those wicked" farmers objected to their farms being split up. Why shouldn't they fight to protect their heritage? The grading of the land is quite misleading, but the way it is farmed makes it valuable agricultural land and, more important, of a very high quality amenity value, especially when viewed from the moor. No land is sacrosanct—neither that to the north nor to the south of the town—but the considered view of the majority was that the southern route would be less damaging than that to the north.

I believe the alternatives are quite plain—either to accept the decisions reached through the democratic process: build a southern by-pass to a high standard by careful planning and landscaping, protecting residences near the route by screening, double-glazing etc., and accept the land much greater in area than the part of Bluebell Woods required or, a distressing thought, to start at square one with its processes of an initial investigation of possible routes, then public consultation, and eventually the declaration of a preferred route, and another public inquiry at which those affected will oppose the proposal.

Eventually, a decision and construction—judging by past progress this could well be 10 years. More residential development is in hand to the north and north-east of the town, and adds weight to the opposition to a northern by-pass.

The Noble Lords, the petitioners and the member for the South Hams have not been evident in Okehampton to see just how bad the traffic is. Some, no doubt, avoid the town and its traffic queues. Come and meet us and see for yourselves. We live in intolerable conditions.

Then stand at the top of Okehampton Park. Visualise a southern by-pass in the cutting below you, not interfering with the glorious view right out over North Devon and Exmoor. Then visualise a northern by-pass as it runs through the green fields and woodlands of rural Devon; much more damaging and very visible.

Taking a balanced view, to which I have a perfect right, I hope the gods have heard the cry from Okehampton for a by-pass and that it will be built without delay along the route declared in the decision of the Minister, for the safety and benefit of the people who live in and visit Okehampton, to encourage development and creation of jobs in West Devon and Cornwall—and to make the travellers' journey a safer one.

Walter Passmore
Five times Mayor of Okehampton

H.R.H. Princess Anne on a recent visit to the West Country.

Truro Cathedral enveloped in a snow storm.

The round houses of Veryan keeping out the devil.
Photo: Bob Roskrow

The beach after a storm

Walking a gale-swept seashore in winter can be quite an experience. When the great winds blow shorewards, mountainous waves bulldoze deep into the beach and reveal the rich variety of life that in summer lived deep beneath the deckchairs.

Tens of thousands of grey otter shells, each half the size of a saucer, lie dying in the cold air.

Herring gulls pick them up and rise to a hundred feet before releasing the shell which hurtles down to shatter on the hard sand. And the gull feeds.

I have seen drifts of red nose cockles 100 yards long by 50 yards wide, in places two feet deep. Among this sad, wasted mass of dying animals, an occasional cockle twists its red foot and makes its tortuous way back to the sea.

Here too are the 10-inch long razorfish shells. Wading among them, anglers gather bait for many a fishing trip. When freshly dug, their succulent white flesh dipped in oatmeal and lightly cooked, is the most delicate of seafoods.

Here flocks of gulls gather at the edge of the surf: herring gulls, lesser and great black backs, black-headed gulls and occasional rarities. Every one drawn to the feast.

Yet even hungry gulls avoid sea mice. Shaped like flattened courgettes, their grey bodies are covered with rainbow-hued hairs. How strange that such a beautiful worm should spend its days buried in the mud of the seabed.

Grey, grape-like egg masses of whelks lie beside mermaids' purses. These latter, the egg capsules of the dogfish, are "home" for the embryo during its seven month growth period.

Among the spume lie brilliant sunset shells, queen shells in many colours, cowries, troughs, tellins and the intricately carved sting winkle and pelican's foot.

Such a prodigal waste of life. Yet next year as many again may be stranded here on the beach.

Leslie Jackman

How Jim came into journalism

I first came under the influence of The Western Morning News more than 50 years ago. I was a reluctant apprentice reporter on a local weekly. I hated it. My mind was on the mysteries of radio, then in its early commercial stages.

I was a short-wave addict. Amateur radio "hams" used to call me up on Sunday mornings. I couldn't reply, but the rapture of those calls from 6WT—Dr. Wortley-Talbot, of Torquay—and 5TZ, old "Jumbo" from the Isle of Wight, were indescribable.

But here I was on my father's orders, bound to the editor of a weekly newspaper for a penal period of four years and doomed, it seemed to me, to spend the rest of my life standing at country church-gates taking the names of "general" mourners.

One man changed that. Fred. T. Cole was the local representative for The Western Morning News. Short, spry, almost birdlike in his movements, Fred was allowed to write "stories". That may seem ridiculous to modern journalists who spend their lives writing what are known in the trade as "stories" but in those far-off days weekly reporters, especially apprentices, were shorthand writers first and foremost. All that was demanded of us was that we should report funerals, jumble sales, weddings and if we were particularly talented, parish council meetings. It took me three years to get to parish council status.

But Freddie Cole presented me with a vision. He worked a 12-hour day, never going home until he had done his final police call at around 10.15 p.m. True, Freddie combined this slave labour with the more enjoyable task of standing at the bar. That rather exclusive little hostelry known as Sam Denning's was his favourite watering hole.

Sometimes when it came to 'phoning his last bit of copy about 10 p.m. Freddie was beginning to twitch his shoulders a little—a sure sign that he was approaching his quota. But I only remember him once allowing his devotion to The Western Morning News to be impeded and that was when we found him imparting a message to an annoyed and frustrated copytaker at the Plymouth office that "Mr. Stone's dead—stone dead".

Nevertheless we all revered Freddie as the epitome of a then modern journalist. He used to farm out some of his work to help us apprentices who were on a rising scale starting at four shillings a week—20p in modern currency—rising by annual increments of 5p to 50p a week.

I think The Western Morning News allowed him to pay us a shilling a job plus a half-penny a mile expenses. My first job for Freddie was the Wednesday night greyhound meeting at the local rugby football ground.

The fact that I was being paid an extra sum equal to one-fourth of my weekly income did not impress me. It was the carefully concealed pride that I felt as I asked for the Plymouth number and said "Copy please" with as authoritative voice as I could muster at 17. Then the joy of opening The Western Morning News next morning and seeing my, yes my, greyhound results on the sports page. What bliss.

Then the chief reporter Jimmy Lemon would cut into my reverie. "There's a big funeral at Bratton Fleming this afternoon. Better get there early and check whether they want the wreaths in." So off I would go on my unwieldy French push-bike with its high frame and small wheels to stand outside the church taking names from mumbling country-folk who were nevertheless desperately eager to see their name in the paper.

Long after I had completed my apprenticeship and moved away, Freddie Cole's influence dominated my working life-style. The Western Morning News was the one paper I wanted to work for.

I first started to work for The Western Morning News on demobilisation. I combined the duties of chief reporter of the Tiverton Gazette with representing The Western Morning News in that area. Fortunately Tiverton was a compact town. Nightly "calls" could be done easily on a push-bike, but like Freddie Cole, I rarely finished before 10 p.m.

It is strange how journalistic fashions change. "Bright" reporting was looked upon with suspicion. Speed and accuracy were of paramount importance. Any reporter who left a council meeting, or a police court, without his "copy" being written up all ready for the sub-editors was a cissy. Typewriters were for features and such like.

I was completely indoctrinated into the Morning News system by the time that, for family reasons, I left Tiverton and moved in 1949 back to my home town of Barnstaple to look after, from a general news angle, a slice of territory stretching from just above Bude to

Porlock in Somerset.

I did this single-handed at first, but when my wife kept telling me that I only had a night off on Saturdays and I was working seven days a week—Sunday in the summer was the busiest day of the week with all the cricket and beach fatalities to do—the Morning News sent me an assistant who, alas, died at an early age.

He was succeeded by David Mudd, now MP for a Cornish constituency. I am sure David will not dispute that he was more devoted to organising dances with big-name bands than sitting in the Press seats at council meetings and police courts.

Eventually there arrived on the scene Terry Fleet from the Dartmouth Chronicle, a remarkable young journalist who eventually became programme head at Westward Television, but to everyone's grief died comparatively young.

But what was happening to me? I had become hopelessly addicted to the almost fatal conviction that whatever happened the Morning News had to be first. I was the first journalist to reach Lynmouth on the morning of the flood disaster, having ploughed through water nearly two-feet deep on my little James 125 cc motor-cycle.

Motorbike fans have told me that was impossible but the fact is I did it. I spent six weeks motor-cycling between Barnstaple and Lynmouth sharing the work with a young WMN reporter sent up from Plymouth who had a little Velocette motor-cycle. We used to meet at a spot known as Zig-Zag and exchange progress reports.

When after some time as behind-the-scenes deputy agricultural writer for the Morning News I was appointed by Noel A. T. Vinson, the then editor, in a three-line communication, the official agricultural correspondent, life changed.

I even began to attend agricultural functions like the Royal Show. I regularly journeyed to London to report important Min of Ag events such as the annual price review.

I even got official sanction to "cover" the Paris agricultural show. And, of course, I used to go on European jamborees at the invitation of the EEC and various multi-national chemical firms like Ciba-Geigy. But they were strictly "on the house" and I rarely even changed my few pounds sterling into local currency.

During nearly a quarter of a century as agricultural correspondent I learned how the WMN had been built into the mental infrastructure of the South-West. In Cornwall they called it "the paper."

Even at this late stage I feel that, like the lifebelts we used to wear at all times when at sea during the war, if I am divested of an association which has weathered the storms and the rewards of nearly 40 years and a journalistic career stretching back more than half-a-century, I shall quickly sink and become just a momentary bubble on the surface of the sea of time.

Jim Butcher

Pilchards come back in Cornwall

Pilchards, the traditional fish of Cornwall, are being landed in quantities again at Newlyn harbour. Yesterday, skipper Mr. Michael Hosking of Porthleven put 60 tonnes ashore from his 100 foot pelagic trawler Silver Harvester.

After the ban imposed on mackerel fishing inside the South-West "box" these catches have come at the right time for fishermen—and local canners.

The Silver Harvester has landed about 260 tonnes this year.

There was a time when dozens of boats took part in the Mount's Bay pilchard fishing—and when enormous catches were landed. Those years have gone—and so had the pilchards, said the experts—but Mr. Hosking and his crew have caught their latest hauls off the Eddystone.

"We are not allowed to catch mackerel in an area stretching from about 50 miles south of Land's End to 130 miles east of The Lizard," he said yesterday during a lunchtime break on board, alongside Newlyn's new pier.

"So we have turned to pilchards, and they are there. They are for Shippams of Chichester with the processing and freezing being carried out here."

There were a few mackerel in the catch: only 20 stone in the 60 tonnes.

"We are the only Cornish boat involved in this at the moment, except for the driftnet boats, and we are planning to carry on until the end of February," said Mr. Hosking.

"There are some heavy shoals around and nobody has been fishing them for years."

Twenty years ago Mr. Hosking fished in the same area with the old-fashioned pilchard drift nets.

"The pilchards are certainly getting us out of a very difficult situation at the present time. We either do that . . . or get out," he said.

Mr. Dennis Cook, Shippams Ltd. manager at Newlyn and Penzance, said the catches would be used in fishpaste manufacture at Chichester and also processed locally for coldstore at Long Rock for future canning at Newlyn. Both mackerel and pilchards are canned here.

"The question mark is over next winter's mackerel. We had supplies until the new year and put away most of 1985's requirements into coldstore," he said.

"What happens next winter is another matter."

Douglas Williams

The experts in South Armagh

The 800 men of the 1st Battalion, The Devonshire and Dorset Regiment, on its seventh tour of duty since 1970, have been based at Abercorn Barracks, some 30 miles from Belfast, for the last two years.

Many share camp life with wives and children in the self-contained, even isolated, community of 2,000 people. All share the sense of belonging that comes from being the pride of the Westcountry, drawing 90 per cent of its recruits from the two counties.

"It gives a sense of identity and a common way of thought. The Westcountry does things in a certain way. The men have a common background," said battalion commander Lt.-Colonel Bryan Dutton.

The regiment's cohesive family spirit, only heightened by the tension of duty, sharply contrasts with the division that has plagued the surrounding community for three centuries. And yet, the South Armagh countryside, where "Janners" [the nickname for the Devons' men] spend five weeks at a time on patrolling operations, is strangely reminiscent of the South-West.

A two-year tour, supporting a series of other battalions spending only four months in the province, has given the Devon and Dorsets a special on-the-ground knowledge of the area and the people in it.

"We are the South Armagh experts," says Col. Dutton proudly, pointing to the valuable experience, intelligence and continuity a long stay can provide.

"After all, the terrorist fights the war year after year, not in four-month cycles.

"What we are doing is dealing even-handedly with terrorism within the law. Our aim is to continue to help take out terrorists for them to be locked up through the due legal process so that ultimately the politicians will come to a solution."

As the regiment prepares to pack for a move to Germany, Col. Dutton will not be drawn on hopes for the future of the Northern Ireland his men will leave behind.

There are no parade-ground dictators at Ballykinler; drill isn't a requirement for South Armagh and training is fitted in with operational demands.

But Berlin is the next stop, a showcase requiring different skills and organisation, all of which has to be planned. As 345 families, including hundreds of children, look forward to new homes in a new country, posters proclaim "Germany is Wunderbar".

The strength behind the community spirit is the community of wives, not just from the Westcountry, but also from Colchester, Germany, Malta and other places the regiment has been.

For single men, relaxation is possible in local pubs and discos, although all would be wary about where they choose for a night out. Nevertheless, several have Irish girlfriends.

Links with relatives, friends and loved ones back in the Westcountry are important—the delivery tomorrow of 1,000 pasties, organised by Plymouth Junior Chamber of Commerce, is eagerly awaited.

Greg Hatfield

Snow on the farm

Fortunately we had got all the livestock under cover before the driving snow, that was supposed to be falling on London, hit us. Even so, it created the usual innumerable problems, particularly as it followed some remarkably heavy frosts. All the usual farm tasks take twice as long when one has to wade through deep snow from building to building.

The deepest drifts always seem to collect in front of a door of a shed containing a piece of equipment one hasn't used for weeks, but is desperately needed today. Also there is always at least one nasty surprise.

Going into the big barn for a bale of hay, I discovered that the whole top of the stacks looked to have been covered with icing sugar. The wind had been in exactly the right direction to drift a liberal quantity of snow under the roof slates and onto the hay. No great harm done when the snow was still dry, but it would have done no good at all if it melted. So there was nothing for it but to clamber on to the top of the stack of bales and brush off all the snow with a yard broom.

Snow drifting into our lane made it impossible for cars, but negotiable by tractor, to reach our minor road. No milk lorries could reach farms but several farmers set out with tractor and trailer to take their milk several miles to the nearest town in the hope that milk transporters could meet them there. The extra toil and disruption can be imagined when it is remembered that milk is transported these days by tankers, which syphon it from bulk tanks filled directly from the milking machines on each farm. So, each farmer would have had to use extemporary containers for his milk.

At least so far it has not been as bad of the winter of 1962–63. Then, for several weeks, I took my churns by tractor many miles to a pick-up point on the nearest trunk road. I was confident that below the hard packed snowdrifts I was traversing, was the tarmacadam of our local B road. It was only when the thaw came that I discovered I had actually been driving on top of a hedge!

By this afternoon, the snow plough had made two passes along our road, opening it up for some motor traffic. As always, I was filled with admiration for the work done by these council snow clearance teams. I suppose a farmer, having to cope with the stuff himself, realises what a cold frustrating job it can be, contending with snow.

The work has to be continuous and the wind has a nasty habit of blowing snow straight back to places from which it has recently been cleared. Inevitably, machinery will break down under the strain—often at night—and then a fitter has to crawl underneath and bare his hands to metal that is at a low enough temperature for ordinary diesel oil to freeze.

Yet, whenever bad weather causes some chaos, there is always a howl by critics asking: "Why are we not prepared?" They seem to think that provision must be made to deal with every road in the county simultaneously for at least five months of every year. As has recently been shown, our climate is totally unpredictable and instant cover everywhere is impossible except at a cost which could only come from a huge increase in taxation.

We should be grateful for the well organised teams drawn from the basic council workforce that react remarkably well to emergencies. Critics might try a little self-help and motorists in particular should drive with more competence and consideration.

Bob Holmes

Good sermon

I went to church last Sunday and I might go more often if every preacher delivered as good a sermon as the one I heard.

In this case the preacher was rather a distinguished one, Bishop Michael Mann, Dean of Windsor, who is in effect the Queen's vicar. He was preaching at the centenary of Sparkwell Parish Church, a mile or two from Plympton, and he was there because he was once vicar of Sparkwell.

He told a delightful anecdote of how he was trying to explain women's lib to an old gentleman at Exeter who heard him out patiently and then commented, "Well, my old lady thinks she wears the trousers but I supply the braces."

John Theobald

Wood to keep you warm

Everybody loves a wood fire in the hearth. "Partly, perhaps," as Sir Stephen Tallents said, "the love is inherited. Our ancestors, near or remote, had nothing but wood to warm them; and the sight and scent of a wood fire may well stir long-buried racial memories. No other fire lends such a variety of colour to its flames, casts such dancing shadows, breathes such fragrant scents, dies into so clean an ash."

For those who seek to sit warm and enlivened by a successful wood fire this winter, here are a few seasoned tips on managing a forest fire indoors.

Oak is commonly rated the best wood fuel, but it needs to be old and dry. It is of course slow to season, but at its best burns slowly and with intense heat, although if any of its smoke escapes from the grate this may be slightly irritating to the eyes and throat.

Elm was until recently a rather under-appreciated wood, partly because it was less than commonly found. Now, thanks alas to the spread of elm disease, more elm logs may be available in some areas. They should be burnt as soon as possible. Elm makes a good fuel, very hot and tenacious, sometimes as an old Devon rhyme has it, "like smouldering flax, no flames to be seen."

Beech is for many people the best all-round fuel and is usually plentiful, at least in the southern half of Britain. For best results, again, beech logs need to be dry and well seasoned, otherwise they may prove slow to ignite.

Chestnut logs of both the horse and sweet varieties are often offered, especially by travelling sellers, but they are poor fuels, often burning "scarce at all," or else throwing out clouds of dangerous sparks and little else.

Hawthorn is sworn by many countrymen to be the best wood of all to burn—if you can get it. If cut early in the autumn, hawthorn logs will certainly offer the highest density of heat for weight of wood burnt, flaming away in spite of their greenness like good coal.

This value-for-money angle is important if you burn a lot of wood: remember always that, in proportion, a ton of wood takes up as much storage space as two or two-and-a-half tons of coal.

Birch burns too fast for everyday use but, for the occasional fiery display in your hearth, burn some logs of white or silver birch still bearing their satiny bark. They will provide a dazzling clear light and fierce heat, like clean flaming oil and quite different from the heavy flatness of burning pine.

Walnut, if you come across any, is excellent, and the brittle twigs make good fragrant kindling.

Willow is sold widely in some parts, but it is a poor fuel on its own, sparking dangerously. If mixed with larger logs of heavier woods, however, it has its use.

Larch will make the liveliest fire of all the conifer woods, but be ready for splutters and sparks, preferably with a fine-mesh fireguard always left in place when the room is empty.

Apple and cherry logs are of course delightful, giving off good heat and smelling "like flowers in bloom."

Finally, of the commonly available logs, there is ash. Not too long in seasoning, burning powerfully when green or dry, ash logs "all smooth and grey" make superb fuel, and have long been acclaimed as "fit for a queen to warm her slippers by."

As the already-quoted old country rhyme advises, "Buy up all that comes your way, They're worth their weight in gold."

Certain woods possess peculiarly attractive beauty when burning. The resinous pines give their intense blazing flames and an incense-like odour to match. Best of all for the latter is juniper, with its tiny filmy smoke.

Cedar logs also give a lovely aromatic smell when burning, while cherry logs provide multi-coloured flames of great interest. If your apple logs are really old they will burn with a serene brightness, canary yellow, pale blue and saffron tints shifting and flickering.

Arrange your logs in the grate so that they always, as old countrymen say, "kiss one another." Don't make the mistake of poking a wood fire a lot thinking that makes it burn more briskly.

Two logs placed parallel fashion side by side, with a few coals in between, will make their own draught, which comes in at the end of each log. Moreover, they will retain the increasing heat between themselves, constantly adding to it by reflecting heat from one to the other.

Experiment constantly all you can, mixing woods freely, using up twigs and dry bark as kindling, chunks of old rotting wood to add colourful delight to a well-established fire, trying anything once. I once burnt some old privet logs, and found them almost as good as oak, giving out intense heat and leaving almost no ash.

For special occasions it is possible actually to colour the flames in your wood fire to order. Some old rusty nails will provide reddish-purple flames, and a pinch or two of copper sulphate crystals will give you the bluest flames you could wish for.

Old pieces of wood or pine cones soaked in a simple solution of one pound of boric acid to one gallon of water, then dried well in a warm room, will provide delightful green flames when added to the fire. Orange peel, too, makes some colourful effects, chiefly bluish.

And if you want a really heady scent to fill your room, if not your entire house, try adding some dry sticks of old lavender.

Good burning!

David Gunston

The world's loudest woman

She is quite simply the loudest woman on earth. She loves the description and revels in her entry in the Guinness Book of Records. She believes life is one huge laugh and prides herself on seeing a joke in every situation. She is Grace Hall of Tedburn St. Mary, Town Crier extraordinary.

Grace has won world-wide recognition for her enormous voice. Her 112 decibel shout has been broadcast throughout Australia and America. She is a tiny woman with an infectious laugh and twinkling eyes. She says she does everything for fun.

"I'm a natural clown, I can't help it," she says. "My whole life is a series of laughs. When I see people in the street I always want to say something idiotic. Then they say 'Darling you've made my day' because I can make 'em laugh!"

She was only in her teens when she realised she had an exceptional voice.

"I went for my first singing lessons with Signor Dante Coraigni who had just come to London from the Italian Conservatoire of Music," she says.

"He listened to me singing and I have never seen such an expression of horror on a human face. When I'd finished he said: 'That is the most terrible voice I have ever heard in all my life. What on earth have you been doing?'

"I said I sing some songs with my deep voice, and some soprano songs with my top voice, and there you are. He said: 'If you want me to teach you, you will sing the twelve notes that bridge those two voices only, for two years. If you are prepared to do this, I will take you on!' "

Grace did just that. She trained for five years on the twelve notes until she could bridge the two voices and sing through three octaves. The Italian Master then wanted her to sing in Grand Opera. But when she went to Covent Garden she decided it was not for her.

Instead she went "on the boards"—joined a variety show and toured the country. Among people she toured with was Lancashire lass Gracie Fields who, Grace claims, cut off all her hair because of jealousy.

"It has never grown properly since," she says. "That's why I always wear a wig."

The wig and town crier's lace-trimmed scarlet regalia are all part of the comical image Grace now likes to project. She got the outfit from a theatrical costumier but added the fancy trimmings herself, topping the outfit with a cocked hat and an ostrich feather.

Photos of her dressed in her gear adorn the walls of her neat caravan home in the Pathfinder Village, Tedburn St. Mary.

She got into the Guinness Book of Records with a shout recorded in the Pathfinder Village. But, she says, two years ago, an American TV company sent a team across to record her, and they reckoned she exceeded 110 decibels, so they sent her to Heathrow Airport to yell at Concorde.

"Concorde idles at 112 decibels which is what I had reached by then," she says. "It is that yell which went all over the world. People have written to me saying they are in fits of laughter about this funny female who can make as much noise as Concorde."

Peggy Archer

Parable of the scalded leg

I always find Christmas a little confusing. It is the most widely observed religious festival of the year and at the same time almost a pagan revel. One can stumble through the darkness to a village church ablaze with candlelight having spent most of the day avoiding the drunks.

It has probably always been like this. When Christ was born, the innkeeper at Bethlehem wisely put Mary in the stable. She was safer there, away from the noisy pilgrims having a quick drink on the way to Jerusalem, some five miles down the hill.

And for centuries, the Christians refused to celebrate Christ's birth publicly, lest it be confused with the Roman Saturnalia, their pagan feast for the New Year. Christian people preferred to slip away quietly to a mass of their own, where the story was read and the bread and wine shared privately.

Gradually, as the Church became more powerful, the universal mid-winter holiday gained a new meaning as the idea of Christmas took over. Carols, Christmas trees, cards and turkeys are all quite recent additions to the original idea of celebrating the simplicity of Christ's arrival on this planet. And it is not always easy to sort out the real from the rubbish. Piety and revelry have been thoroughly mixed up.

All that said, I am sure that the universal popularity of Christmas springs from deep human feeling. Once a year we want to gather our families and friends together and let generous hospitality overtake the rigours of the day-to-day struggle to make ends meet.

Once a year we want to tell each other that God, if there is a God out there, understands ordinary people and was prepared to share our life. Once a year we want to find some reason beyond ourselves for hoping that real peace may come to the world.

And once a year we want our fickle faith stirred by the reminder that God intends to bring us to Himself. Simply put, every Christmas we want His light to shine out of the darkness that otherwise surrounds us.

To hold on to such hopes at Christmas these days may sound like romantic nonsense. Violence, war, destruction and death haunt our confused world as they always have. Nevertheless, out of these things the truth of Christmas can be made clearer.

I once asked some children to write and act a short Christmas play. Mostly they produced simple scenes of shepherds, cattle and cribs.

But one group set their play in the kitchen. At the crucial moment, mother dropped the turkey out of the oven and the boiling fat scalded her leg. She went to hospital and the rest of the family struggled to turn their tragedy into a deeper love for each other. That group of children had hammered out what Christmas really meant.

So what are we to do about the confusion of Christmas? Perhaps we are heading for a sharper separation between religious and secular ways of keeping the feast. Perhaps the Church's message would have a sharper impact if it were made distinct from the general goodwill of the season.

The danger of that, it seems to me, is making God too small, the private property of the few believers. There is another more generous way, which I can best describe in a little parable.

Last evening I stood on the cliffs at Sidmouth staring out to sea. In the gloom a light suddenly flashed and the horizon became clear, then it was gone. Again it flashed and was immediately lost in the rain. Still I had seen it, and so could other people, intermittently.

It seems to me that the Christmas light should go on shining for everyone to see.

The Rt. Rev. Peter Coleman
Bishop of Crediton

Energetic workforce

Walking across a field, I felt the ground give slightly under my feet. Looking down, I could see the turf was raised slightly in a straight line running from the nearest bank to a point where a pipe carried water from an underground spring to the nearest ditch.

Closer examination showed that my foot had crushed the roof of an underground tunnel, very obviously the work of a mole.

I opened up a short section to reveal that the run looked well polished, indicating that it was in regular use, probably by more than one animal. Moles are great drinkers and it was obvious that the underground spring was their regular water supply.

It is commonly assumed that the pushed up cones of earth we see in the field and call molehills indicate a place that moles regularly visit.

In fact, they are only surplus mounds of earth pushed up by moles when hunting for worms and grubs near the surface.

Their main runs, connecting breeding sites in hedges, water supplies and feeding grounds, are much deeper and can only be detected in those places where hard ground or rock forces the diggers near the surface. These were the runs sought by the old mole catchers who trapped these creatures for a living.

Wonderfully equipped for digging, with front feet like shovels, a mole can dig itself out of sight in seconds. Its marvellous sense of smell enables it to catch a sufficiently large quantity of prey to fuel its energetic performance.

Frost never penetrates its hunting grounds, so it has no need to hibernate.

The moles' underground workings provide a valuable form of field drainage. Farmers have copied it by using a so called mole plough with a torpedo shaped coulter that creates underground tunnels, similar to those made by moles.

Whenever I carry out this operation, I find that my moles soon gratefully adopt some of these artificial runs for their own use.

Bob Holmes